Stressing that the nine countries have widely varying problems of modernization to overcome, the author of this book points out that in many ways the leaders tend to work towards similar solutions: strong central governments, one party domination, acceptance of foreign assistance and capital, and above all, jealous defense of independence.

———————————   ——————————

JOHN D. HARGREAVES, author of this volume in the Modern Nations in Historical Perspective series, is Professor of History at the University of Aberdeen, Scotland, and from 1952-1954 was Senior Lecturer in History at Fourah Bay College, Sierra Leone. He is the author of *Prelude to the Partition of West Africa* and the chapter on "European Relations in Africa, 1763-93" in the *New Cambridge Modern History,* along with numerous articles in scholarly journals.

THE MODERN NATIONS IN
HISTORICAL PERSPECTIVE

ROBIN W. WINKS, *General Editor*

The volumes in this series deal with individual
nations or groups of closely related nations
throughout the world, summarizing the chief historical trends and influences that have contributed
to each nation's present-day character, problems,
and behavior. Recent data are incorporated with
established historical background to achieve a
fresh synthesis and original interpretation.

JOHN D. HARGREAVES has been Professor of History and Head of Department in the University
of Aberdeen since 1962. His interests began to
extend from European into African History in
1952-54, when he was Senior Lecturer in History
at Fourah Bay College, Sierra Leone. His publications include A *Life of Sir Samuel Lewis* and
Prelude to the Partition of West Africa.

ALSO IN THE AFRICAN SUBSERIES

Central Africa *by Prosser Gifford*
The Congo *by Harry R. Rudin*
Egypt & the Sudan *by Robert Collins and Robert Tignor*
Ethiopia, Eritrea & the Somalilands *by William H. Lewis*
Morocco, Algeria, Tunisia *by Richard M. Brace*
Nigeria & Ghana *by John E. Flint*
Portuguese Africa *by Ronald Chilcote*
Sierra Leone and Liberia *by Christopher Fyfe*

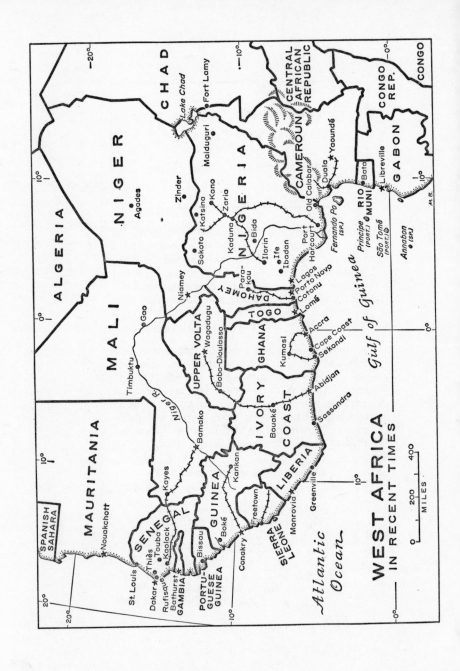

WEST AFRICA
IN RECENT TIMES

WEST AFRICA: THE FORMER FRENCH STATES

JOHN D. HARGREAVES

A SPECTRUM BOOK

Prentice-Hall, Inc.
Englewood Cliffs, New Jersey

Current printing (last number):

10   9   8   7   6   5   4   3   2   1

PREFACE

It is not easy to write a short introduction to the history of nine states which, although they have passed through important experiences in common, retain marked individual characteristics. This is, I believe, the first time the task has been attempted in quite this form in any language. I have therefore tried to support the interpretative discussion appropriate to this series with reasonably full references to the authorities and evidence I have used. Perceptive readers will observe how much remains to be verified and discovered. I hope they will contribute to these processes.

No author can write a work like this without incurring many obligations. One of the greatest is owed to the University of Aberdeen, especially to its Library staff. Among other libraries where I have been helped to work I should single out that of the Royal Commonwealth Society, London. My Secretary, Ann Gordon, has done invaluable work in preparing the manuscript, her judgment and discrimination being almost equal to her patience. Sheila, Sara, Catherine, and Alastair Hargreaves have in their various ways contributed to this, as they do to all my enterprises.

Mr. Iain MacIver assisted me during the writing of Chapter Six, supported by a grant from the Carnegie Trust for the Universities of Scotland under their admirable scheme for promoting undergraduate research. During the later stages of my work I was enabled to pay brief visits to Senegal and Mali by a generous grant from the British Council. In Dakar I enjoyed assistance and hospitality from many quarters, especially from Jean-François Maurel, the archivist, and from Vincent Monteil, Director of the Institut Français d'Afrique Noire. Among the friends who have helped to improve my work by their advice, or comments on parts of the manuscript, are Michael Crowder (who during my short visit to Freetown, and subsequently, found time to make very extensive criticisms), Roy Bridges, Christopher Fyfe, H. O. Idowu, Roger Pasquier, and Yves Person. Other academic debts are acknowledged in footnotes. The responsibility for the remaining errors is of course my own.

J.D.H.

ABBREVIATIONS USED IN REFERENCES

Archive Repositories

AAOF   Archives, former French West Africa (Dakar).

ANSOM   Archives Nationales, Section d'Outre-Mer. Rue Oudinot (Paris).

PRO.   Public Record Office, Chancery Lane (London).

Periodicals

BCEHSAOF   *Bulletin,* Comité d'Etudes Historiques et Scientifiques de l'Afrique Occidentale française. (Dakar).

CEA   *Cahiers d'Etudes Africaines* (Paris).

IFAN.   Publications of l'institut français d'Afrique Noire, Dakar (now the Institut *Fondamentale* d'Afrique Noire).

JAH   *Journal of African History* (London).

JHSN   *Journal,* Historical Society of Nigeria (Ibadan).

JMAS   *Journal of Modern African Studies* (London).

CONTENTS

ONE

NINE STATES

When a student of the contemporary world seeks to distinguish patterns or affinities among the thirty to forty sovereign African states which are currently represented in the United Nations, he may well be puzzled about the principles appropriate to such an enquiry. On the whole he would not be well-advised to read too much significance into voting patterns or other temporary alignments which may emerge from time to time over international issues. In 1961 many people thought they had discovered a decisive clue in the emergence of the "Casablanca" group of states—variously described as radical, neutralist, Leftist—and the "Monrovia" group, dubbed as "moderate," pro-western, conservative, imperialist-dominated, or with whatever other adjectives seemed most accurately to express the reaction of the observer. And at the time of the international meetings referred to, these distinctions were important. But they did not prove profound or long-lasting. By the time the Addis Ababa conference met in May 1963 to found the Organization of African Unity the end of the Algerian war had relieved one major tension experienced by African states which still depended heavily on French aid; conservatives and radicals were able to unite in a statement of anti-imperialist intentions considerably more drastic than the "radical" Casablanca resolutions of 1961. Subsequent international disputes have from time to time led the "radicals" to stand up to be counted; but the tally has not always been the same. Over Rhodesia, for example, two of the "Monrovia" powers (Mauritania and Congo-Brazzaville) broke off relations with the United Kingdom in December 1965, and others used strong language in the O.A.U.; two of the "Casablanca" group (Morocco and Libya) failed to do so. Few African states are neutral on the issues of decolonization; their radicalism is a matter of degree and circumstance.

1

The scholar seeking a scheme of classification, baffled by this apparent incoherence in contemporary politics, may be tempted to go far back in time to seek distinctions of a less mutable nature. And this may be more fruitful. Just as in Europe it has been found useful to distinguish groups of states according to the language spoken (or, more dubiously, according to the ethnic origin of their people) so may interesting results be obtained by asking similar questions in Africa. Comparative philological studies, even examination of the distribution of certain types of blood, permit us to establish similarities of considerable importance for academic students of African history and ethnology. And in some cases observed affinities (among Arabic-speakers or Somalis or Bakongo) may provide vital clues to the understanding of contemporary affairs. Yet, as we would expect from the analogy with Europe, all these examples are of rather particular, localized, importance. (Scandinavia may have considerable cultural unity, but Sweden does not join Norway and Denmark in NATO). And it is doubtful how far the larger cultural unities which scholars may discover—those based on attitudes to cattle, or on rice-growing, or even on the Bantu group of languages—represent important facts of contemporary political geography.

Where then should the larger unities of modern Africa be sought? Historians, like other specialists, are tempted to answer in ways which seem to place a premium on their own methods of study. There is a range of "national characteristics"—less broad and general than those observed by ethnographers or anthropologists, less ephemeral than those noted by reporters in the conference halls—which may (in principle) be traced to common experiences of the nation within its remembered past. Some of the most profound of the historical experiences which differentiate African peoples have operated over many centuries. Lands with long experience of Islamic government share important resemblances of institutions and culture; so do districts on the Atlantic coast which have long engaged in Atlantic trade. Yet the differences within such groupings are even more pronounced.

For most African states, the most recent and powerful collective experience has been that of colonial rule. European powers determined or consolidated the political boundaries; provided the present *linguae francae* of the educated men; influenced the outlook and behaviour of key groups of Africans (directly or indirectly, positively or negatively) in ways which will affect the culture and customs of whole new nations long after the end of independence celebrations. This essay will survey the history of nine very different states; and many of the forces which it discusses spread far beyond the modern boundaries. What unites these states as a feasible (if not wholly satisfactory) unit of study is simply their common experience of French rule, even though, at its termination, this had extended beyond the memory of octogenarians only in a few small districts. Leopold Sédar-Senghor, President of Senegal, considers that this experience may prove sufficient to make nations of these peoples.

> What makes the Nation is the common will to live together. Generally this common will derives from history, and from being neighbours—not necessarily good neighbours. Now the history of the last sixty years has brought us together in the former French West Africa. . . . We cannot swim back against this stream of history without the risk of drowning.[1]

This argument, based on the practical importance of the colonial legacy to contemporary states, provides theoretical justification for treating the French-speaking countries of West Africa as a single unit of study. Its acceptance still leaves the writer with the responsibility of avoiding the temptation to take the line of least resistance by writing colonial history. During the second half of the twentieth century, western historians have at last begun to realize that the history of Africa before "the coming of the white man" is a subject which not only influences the life of contemporary Africans, but is capable of study in genuine academic depth. But the formative influences of this precolonial period rarely followed modern boundary lines; it is necessary to think of West Africa as a whole, or of subregions defined geographically or ethnographically.

At the height of her power in West Africa, France controlled an area the size of Europe without Russia; her Governors-General ruled a wider dominion than any other officials in the history of overseas France. But initially its boundaries had been settled more or less arbitrarily by international agreements that reflected the state of European politics more faithfully than local realities (though these were not totally ignored). Later, it was subdivided into territories which, after further boundary changes, eventually formed the basis

[1] Leopold Sédar-Senghor, *Nation et Voie africaine du Socialisme* (Paris, 1961), p. 113.

of the modern states; administrative convenience was usually the dominant consideration in this process. At each stage frontier posts cut across the guiding lines in the complex pattern of affinities and antagonisms which history had created among West Africans, splitting up many of the 126 language groups which European scholars were later to distinguish in these territories. Above these more or less artificial units there was erected a supraterritorial government, an imposed administrative federation, for all French West Africa (*Afrique Occidentale Française*, or A.O.F.). (Another such government linked the states now known as Gabon, Central African Republic, Congo-Brazzaville, and Chad in *Afrique Equatoriale Française*, or A.E.F.) After World War I portions of two German colonies, Togoland and Kamerun, were brought under French administration as mandated territories, but never incorporated in the "federations" or assimilated to their legal status.[2] The scope of this study includes the eight Republics which until 1958 formed part of A.O.F.: Dahomey, Guinea, Ivory Coast, Mali, Mauritania, Niger, Senegal, Upper Volta; also the former mandate and trust territory of Togo. The equatorial territories and the Republic of Cameroun lie in a geographically distinguishable area, and were subject to different influences in precolonial times. Much, though by no means all, of their colonial experience was comparable to that of the countries to be discussed.

Except for northern Mali and Niger and most of Mauritania, which are in the Sahara desert, these nine states lie within West Africa in the narrower sense of that term: within a region bounded on west and south by the Atlantic, on the north by the desert, on the east, more roughly, by Lake Chad and the mountains of the Cameroons. Inside this great area, geographers identify many separate zones; but the major distinction they make is that between "forest" and "savanna." The forest belt mostly lies south of $7\frac{1}{2}°N$, though along the coast it extends as far north as the Gambia river; it is characterized by its heavy rainfall, and until relatively recent times was in fact largely covered by dense primary forest. Once this is felled the heavy rainfall tends to leach the earth, sweeping precious plant nutrients into the rivers and ocean and leaving infertile, acid soils. In some areas these are dried by the *harmattan* wind into the hard bricklike

[2] For some years after 1934, however, Togo was placed under the Governor of Dahomey and there was some administrative integration between the two territories.

surface, which the Fulas call *bowal* and nongeological Europeans, laterite.

From the northern edges of the forest, annual rainfall decreases progressively up to the borders of the desert and the region known as *sahel*.[3] There is more open grassland (and woodland too); more varied agriculture is possible on soils less harshly treated by the elements. The contract should not be overdrawn. Few savanna soils are naturally rich; wind erosion produces large areas of *bowal*, and variations in weather can easily spoil the year's harvest. But on the whole, until men learned to apply modern science and technology to the African environment, physical conditions seem to have favored the peoples of the savanna above those of the forest in regard to diet, communications, and health.

In the forest, mosquitoes flourished, apparently for many centuries, in swamps and stagnant pools. Different varieties carried malaria and yellow fever which, although populations exposed to them might in time acquire partial immunity, tended (with other diseases) to lower vitality and expectations of life, especially among infants. The tsetse fly, less evenly distributed in the forest, is parasitic on cattle and horses. Because of the trypanosomiasis which it carries(and also because of shortage of pasture) the cattle of the forest belt are even now relatively few, their breeds of small economic value; mixed farming could hardly develop. Moreover, the range of indigenous food-crops was smaller. While rice, millets, and sorghum may have been cultivated in the savanna by the second millennium B.C., it seems likely that most forest peoples relied upon yams and bananas as their staple foods until the introduction of maize and cassava from America in the sixteenth and seventeenth centuries.

That new crops should reach the forest across the ocean from America indicates the poverty of inland facilities for transport and communications. In the savanna, horses, neither killed by the tsetse nor impeded by dense forest, could be used for travel, for transport, and as cavalry mounts. It does not seem that contact was ever difficult between neighboring parts of the region; nor with more distant parts of the world. Caravan routes over the watershed to the Nile valley, across the desert to the Mediterranean, despite their diffi-

---

[3] Savanna and *sahel* together form the area known as the Western Sudan (a conventional narrowing of a term derived from the Arabic phrase *bilad es sudan*, or "land of the Negroes").

culties, have been in continuous use since before the Christian era. But in the forest, human porterage along difficult trails seems to have been the major form of transport until the nineteenth century. True, the area is crossed by many rivers and some of these—the Gambia, the Volta, above all the Niger—were used for the passage of travellers and produce through the forest. But even these, still more the lesser rivers, have only limited value for purposes of transport because of seasonable variations in level, of frequent falls, rapids and shallows, of sandbars and other impediments to access from the sea.

In earlier centuries, as will be seen, certain peoples of the savanna reaped the benefits of their more favored environment. Benefitting from their contacts with other centers of settlement and civilization, in the Nile valley, the Mediterranean, the Near East, they founded states, conducted trade, developed a way of life which commanded respect from all who observed it. But the peoples of the forest have left little record of their development before their societies were stimulated by the growth of oceanic trade. In the five centuries since that trade began, maritime commerce has more than redressed the balance; today the most prosperous and some of the most articulate peoples of Africa live within the west coast forest region. Yet the advance, it should be said, is only relative. Compared with the peoples of Niger, those of Dakar or the southern Ivory Coast may be relatively affluent; compared with citizens of France or the United States, they remain poor. Savanna and forest alike, in varying degrees, fall today into the disturbingly large category of "underdeveloped countries."

What does this term imply in West Africa? Most obviously, low incomes for the people. With the exceptions of Senegal and Ivory Coast, in all these territories the national income per head is estimated to be under $100 a year. The meaning of such figures is difficult to appraise in countries where families produce for themselves a substantial part of the food they eat. Unlike many Asian countries, French-speaking West Africa as a whole still has more than enough land to support its people; though areas like Mossi and south Dahomey, thickly settled in the past for political or military reasons, may yet discover the meaning of overpopulation should economic and technological improvement fail to keep pace with the rising trend of population. Few West Africans starve; but in many districts the "hungry season" is still a grim reality, and almost everywhere diets remain monotonous and poorly balanced. Productive surpluses which might be used for improving conditions of living are severely limited. Although every year sees more concrete houses, more radios, bicycles, sewing machines, the majority of families still lack all these things, and others which in "developed" countries are very widely owned. Public amenities too are severely restricted: railways few, and often antiquated; roads inadequate in mileage, and with rare exceptions in construction also; electrical power available in favored centers only; health services dependent on a few overworked doctors. School-systems still cannot hope to teach all the children (and may not teach the most relevant modern skills, for lack of qualified teachers and of funds).

Descriptions of underdevelopment invariably imply comparisons between African conditions and those in countries termed "developed." The implication is not, as some critics seem to think, that West Africans have never been able to come to terms with their physical environment; but that they have not recently been able to do so in a way which satisfies the increasing expectations of twentieth-century men. Traditional agricultural methods have usually become adapted to the conditions imposed by African soils and climates, and sometimes the overconfident application of western science or techniques has had unfortunate results. Deep ploughing may lay the subsoil open to erosion by rain; the clumsy, short-handed West African hoe or *daba*, it has been argued, breaks up the soil to a more appropriate extent. Long periods of fallow followed by bush-burning—systems of "shifting cultivation," as they are called—restore fertility to the soil as effectively as the application of fertilizers (which are washed away over-rapidly in the rains); only when the population begins to press upon the land does this involve an obviously inefficient use of resources. In districts where density of population makes more intensive cultivation necessary, animal fertilizer has for centuries been provided by arranging for the pasturing of cattle kept by the nomadic Fulas. "Country societies" like the Poro, into which young people are still initiated around the time of puberty provided a prescientific educational system, which—though we know little about it in earlier centuries—clearly bore a fairly close relation to social needs of the people in question.

Certainly, the economies of West Africa seem in recent centuries to have been rather static systems, not prone to starting new developments as a result of internal initiative. (This does not of course mean that there has been no division of labor or exchange of goods; the oldest known description of West African trade is by Herodotus.) But they have proved perfectly capable of change in response to external economic stimuli. During the nineteenth and twentieth centuries the opportunity of producing for overseas markets has led many West African peoples to turn to the commercial production of cash crops—in the 1840s, groundnuts (peanuts) in Senegal and oil-palm in Dahomey, more recently coffee and cocoa in the southern Ivory Coast. But these developments have brought their own problems. Once it has been discovered that a certain crop can be profitably grown in given conditions, commercial pressures may lead to excessive dependence upon it—possibly at the expense of subsistence farming, certainly to the detriment of other possible money-makers. Too many West African countries are dependent for their solvency on a single crop—and sometimes on a single customer for that crop, in this case France. Although in recent years the French government has often agreed to buy African staple exports at guaranteed and favorable prices, in general it remains true that a country's prosperity may vary from year to year according to the success of the season's harvest, the value of the staple in the international market, and the short-term commercial policies of the wholesale merchants who control its exports. Since the most important of these merchants are large European trading companies, it has sometimes appeared that they—together with, in Guinea and more recently Mauritania, foreign mining concerns—have become the effective controllers of the economy. Even if West Africa has never been a really major source of profit to European capitalism, it has long been plausible to argue that European capitalists are getting too much of such profits as there are: that in return for its contributions to the world supply of raw materials, Africa has received only inessential additions to its supply of goods for consumption, not the productive capital with which it could equip itself for growth.

But in recent years the consumption goods, at least, have been flowing back in greater quantity and greater diversity. Some have even flowed back to the peasant producers, others not so far. For foreign rule and foreign capitalism have not prevented, have indeed visibly assisted, the growth of new careers and opportunities open to African talent—in business, administration, the professions. During the last century new ports and seats of government have grown up in many parts of French-speaking West Africa, for the most part where no substantial African town stood formerly; even though founded by and for Europeans, these have become African towns, and here the leaders of the new African states are for the most part to be found. Well-educated and prosperous Africans were not unknown in earlier centuries, especially in Senegal; but only since World War II have they collectively become a major factor in West African life. Now, not only do their incomes enable them to enjoy material standards of life very different from those of their countrymen; their education and experience enables them to enter into the many political economic and technological debates about the future of their countries which have been started by the French and to continue them, translated, in what they claim are more authentically African terms.

Since the end of the 1950s, political leadership in all the French-speaking countries of West Africa has been in the hands of leaders from one section or another of this African educated class, if so it may be called. (The term "middle-class," which has done such long and versatile service to historians of Europe, is perhaps better not exported to Africa.) There are great differences among these leaders, in their personal backgrounds, their political support, their professed aims and ideologies. Modibo Keita of Mali, an austere Muslim intellectual who claims descent from the ancient dynasty of Mali, and Sekou Touré of Guinea, a descendant of the nineteenth-century warrior Samori, who graduated to political leadership through Marxist Trade Unionism, have the reputation of approaching politics as intransigent Jacobins, ready for drastic political and economic measures where these will serve their objectives at home, and are particularly forthright in their denunciations of imperialism abroad. Leopold Sédar-Senghor of Senegal, poet, professor, and political philosopher in the tradition of the most versatile French intellectuals, and Felix Houphouët-Boigny of the Ivory Coast, prosperous planter, *médecin africain* and traditional Baoulé chief, pursue more openly pro-western foreign policies, and are therefore commonly regarded as inherently more "moderate" men. Yet many differences among them can be understood by reference to the effects of the different historical backgrounds of their respective countries on the conditions required for effective political leadership. In the African context, what these men have in common is of greater importance than any of these striking but superficial contrasts of personality and approach.

All recognize, in their countries, the high priority of tasks of economic development, modernization, and diversification. All intend to tackle these problems, to a major extent, by governmental action. All see some danger lest political debate should, in the present condition of African society, turn into sectional or tribal dissension; all have tried to avoid this by moving toward single-party government. This does not necessarily mean that only one party is legal; but in each country the governing party of 1966 holds a dominant position which for one reason or another is unlikely to be successfully challenged at the polls under existing constitutional arrangements. These parties, however, claim to be broadly inclusive bodies, with plenty of room for dissenting opinions if expressed by men of goodwill; and in varying degrees the party organizations do in fact play important roles in mobilizing support and understanding for the government's objectives among the masses of the people. It is misleading to describe any of these states as democracies in any of the specific senses in which that term is usually understood in the United States or western Europe; but by the same criterion it could be misleading to describe them as dictatorships.

In their relations with the outside world, the leaders of all these states acknowledge their need to obtain capital and technical assistance from abroad. They differ in the generosity of the conditions under which they are prepared to accept that capital from the hands of private interests; and in their willingness to risk compromising their independence of action by becoming unduly dependent for publicly controlled capital upon a single foreign government (in practice, France). But all are nevertheless committed before their people to the jealous preservation of that independence. All who were eligible became foundation members of the militant Organization of African Unity set up by the Addis Ababa conference of May 1963; all proclaim their resistance to "neocolonialism" (however they may visualize it), their support of the cause of African unity (by whatever means they seek to further it). Each of these attitudes reflects an interpretation, not only of present realities, but of historical experience.

At this point generalities may conveniently be suspended and some attempt must be made to establish the distinguishing characteristics of the nine states under study. Some of the basic information about these states can be most conveniently presented in tabular form. These figures should be taken with caution—most of those for population represent only rough approximations, and even estimates of area tend to vary—but they do give some indication of relative size, population, and state of development.

Clearly there are significant differences in conditions in these states which a historian should be able not merely to record but to explain. Although the explanation of relative wealth and poverty may partly be found in the lists of mineral and agricultural products which various territories are able to export with profit, natural resources do not explain the whole story. Why should the Voltaic republic be more densely populated than neighboring territories with comparable physical conditions and resources? Why should Senegal have a larger proportion of Europeans in its population than Kenya ever had? Why are Niger and Mauritania so much more solidly Muslim than their neighbor, Mali? Such questions can only be elucidated with the help of particularized historical knowledge; this book aims to provide a guide to the understanding of such differences.

But one general distinction may usefully be made at this stage. Some West African countries have historically been oriented toward the ocean; others, toward the Sahara desert. This distinction corresponds very roughly with that made earlier between the geographer's zones of forest and savanna; but few of the states in question contain only a single type of terrain. It does not provide a water-tight system of classification. Upper Volta does not border either the ocean or the desert, though until recent years it has probably been influenced more strongly from the north than from the south; Guinea, despite its seaboard, has more in common with Mali than with the Ivory Coast; Mauritania, pre-eminently a desert state, will from the 1960s be increasingly influenced by the ocean as it begins to develop its mineral resources. But as a rough guide to the explanation of such figures as those just cited, this distinction between the influence of the ocean and of the desert is as useful as any.

Since the second half of the fifteenth century, the whole West African seaboard has had commercial and cultural contact, in greatly varying degrees of intensity, with merchants and governments in Europe and the Americas. It is very clear that Africa has benefitted from these contacts much less than might reasonably have been hoped; nevertheless it is in countries accessible from the coast that the

SOME COMPARATIVE INDICES

	Senegal	Mali	Mauritania
Est. population, mid-1961 (million)	3.0	4.2	.75
Area (thousand sq. km.)	197	1,204	1,086
Population per sq. km.	15.25	3.5	0.7
Number of foreigners (Europeans?)	53,000	7,100	1,500
Approximate proportion of Muslims	78%	55%	[100%]
Gross National Product, 1961 ($ million)	525	245	
G.N.P. per head ($)	175	58	
Exports, 1961 ($ million)	125	14	1.8
Major exports	Groundnuts and Groundnut oil: Phosphates	Groundnuts	Dried Fish [Iron ore from 1963]
Govt. revenue, 1961 (excl. foreign aid) ($ million)	99	22	5.5
Railways (km.)	1033	640	675 (under construction 1962)
Electrical production, 1960 (kw. million)	127	4.6	0.3 (1958)
Percentage of eligible children enrolled in primary schools, c. 1960	24	8	7
secondary schools c. 1960	2	1	–
Towns over 30,000	Dakar 374,000 Thiès 69,000 Kaolack 67,000 Rufisque 49,000 St. Louis 48,000	Bamako 135,000	–

Many figures represent only approximate estimates, as statistical material on many of these subjects is of doubtful accuracy. The major source is the *Données statistiques* of the Institut National de la Statistique et des Etudes Economiques, Paris, New series No. 2, April-June 1963, supplemented by the special issue of *Europe-France-Outremer* "L'Afrique d'Expression française" (May 1963).

Estimates of Gross National Product and of population are those published by the Agency for International Development, April 30, 1963; those of school enrollment from the United Nations Economic Bulletin for Africa, IV, 1964, pp. 86-7.

impact of these contacts have been chiefly felt. This has provided modest stimuli to economic growth. Thus, in the figures for national income per head of population the Ivory Coast and Senegal are easy leaders, followed by other maritime states, Togo and Guinea. The figures for exports, roads, railways, electrical capacity show comparable tendencies, though with some interesting variations. With school attendance figures it is much the same, though those for Dahomey and Togo reflect a relatively high concentration there of the work

OF POPULATION AND DEVELOPMENT

Guinea	Ivory Coast	Upper Volta	Dahomey	Niger	Togo
3.1	3.4	4.4	2.1	3.1	1.5
[246]	322	274	[112]	1189	57
12.6	10.5	16	18.7	2.6	26.3
	14,500	3,500	2,500	2,700	1,300
65%	15%	17%	17%	85%	5%
185	615	175	80	120	105
60	184	40	40	40	70
62	178	3.6	13	15.5	19
Alumina	Coffee	Livestock	Palm oil	Groundnuts	Coffee
Diamonds	Cocoa		and		and
Bananas	Timber		kernels		cocoa
Coffee					
[36]	114	21	[21]	14	12
662	625	509	579	–	490
13 (1956)	57.2	3.9	5.8 (1958)	6.6	4.2
20	33	7	31	3	32
1	1	–	1	–	1
Conakry	Abijan	Wagadugu	Cotonou	Niamey	Lomé
78,000	124,000	54,000	54,000	30,000	80,000
	Bouaké	Bobo-Dioulasso	Porto-Novo		
	43,000	51,500	31,000		

The approximations for Muslim populations are taken from J. S. Trimingham, *Islam in West Africa* (Oxford, 1959) p. 233.

I have made my own rough conversions to dollars. In a few cases where my basic authority has gaps in its figures I have included, in brackets, an estimate from such unofficial sources as *The Statesman's Year Book*.

of Christian missions. If "progress" in Africa is assumed to mean progress toward the material standards and social conditions of the rich societies of Europe and North America, the oceanic states are in the lead.

On this assumption, it seems to follow that the countries oriented towards the desert—Niger, Mali, Mauritania—are to be regarded as "backward." Thinly populated, not well-endowed with minerals or with suitable conditions for producing lucrative export crops, facing high costs for transport to the ocean ports on which modern commerce depends, they find that their physical location now poses serious problems. But it was not always so. For many centuries caravan routes across the desert were the main highways by which trade goods and ideas from the Mediterranean basin and the world beyond reached West Africa. It was on the edges of the desert that the first great African states developed, supported by the profits of overland trade and enriched by the theological, legal, and scientific ideas of medieval Islam. On these desert frontiers the earliest known African political tradition developed. So it is no accident if it is in Mali and in those coastal states most influenced by this tradition—in Guinea and in different ways in Senegal—that the most radical and articulate assertions of Africa's political and cultural independence are heard today. Things received through the desert still take precedence in many ways over things received across the ocean; it is therefore with a study of this inheritance that a historical study of French-speaking West Africa must begin

Because these nine states are such recent creations, it is unusually difficult to separate the early, precolonial, history of their peoples from that of their neighbors. The Wolof, for example, have a reasonably well-documented history which for the last five centuries lies largely within the borders of modern Senegal, but even their story often overlaps into the Gambia. For earlier periods, less is certain; one African writer tries to establish direct Wolof relationships with classical Egypt. Elsewhere there are much graver difficulties in establishing the origins and ancestry of peoples who today identify themselves by the names of particular ethnic groups.

Indeed, the whole problem of ethnic identity may be extraordinarily complicated. Occasionally it may seem sufficiently established by the inherited physical characteristics of a people like the Fulas; but, in Africa as elsewhere, it is usually necessary to look to acquired, or cultural, characteristics to define differences between peoples. Each ethnic group normally has its own language (though it may not be wholly different from that of its neighbors) and this is probably the most important single determinant; but ethnicity may also be defined by occupation (the Bozos of Mali are fishermen); by historical experience (common resistance to an enemy, assimilation of a conquered people to the culture and language of a ruling group); by religion.

The composition of a group can thus be changed not only by intermarriage but by more or less voluntary decisions comparable to processes of naturalization in more sophisticated legal systems.[4] All this makes it difficult and dangerous to pronounce upon the "origins" of the various African peoples of today. Careful research by historians using oral traditions in conjunction with archaeological, linguistic, and ethnographic evidence is beginning to produce more coherent pictures of the dispersal of African peoples over past centuries, but these findings are still largely tentative, and difficult to summarize concisely in a work on this scale. This book therefore will not discuss problems concerning the early history of particular peoples, but will begin by examining broad themes of African history, whose relevance is not confined to the francophone territories of today. From time to time ethnic names will be applied historically, without necessarily implying complete biological continuity with the peoples who use these names today.

These will not be the only general statements in the book which should be received with critical reserve. Writers of historical surveys often state like established truths propositions which represent merely the most probable of current hypotheses. In the present state of African studies, this is liable to happen rather more often than cautious scholars might desire. The reader is warned.

[4] On this subject, see Jean Gallais, "Signification du groupe ethnique au Mali," *L'Homme,* II (1962), 106-29.

TWO

THE DESERT AND THE SUDAN*

Partly because of certain ambiguities in the common use of the word "history," men are liable to assume that significant social experience begins only with the recording of documentary evidence. In West Africa it is the *sahel* and savanna country between about the 10th and 16th parallels which provides our oldest historical documents; these were mostly written by Muslims in Arabic (or in African languages using Arabic script); hence there is some danger of rejecting the old idea that the significant history of tropical Africa began only with the advent of Europeans in favor of a new but hardly less patronizing view—that it began with the Arabs. Neither view is supported by the evidence which historians are gradually accumulating and critically evaluating in collaboration with archaeologists, philologists, and other specialist students of Africa.

It must be admitted that this evidence remains both difficult and fragmentary; many technical controversies arise which a nonspecialist dare not begin to discuss in a work of this kind. But the general lines of what historians now believe about the early history of the Western Sudan may be briefly and crudely summarized. By the end of the second millennium B.C., much of this country was occupied by settled cultivators, growing millet, rice, and other crops; during the next centuries an indigenous tradition of terra cotta sculpture, of considerable technical and artistic sophistication, began to develop. (This is commonly named after Nok in northern Nigeria, where the first archaeological discoveries were made, but this does not necessarily mean that the style originated there; some French scholars believe that similar work found near Macina may be of earlier date.) By the

---

* Some of the general problems of early West African history which this chapter touches are discussed somewhat more fully in the volume in this series by John E. Flint, *Nigeria and Ghana*, Prentice-Hall, 1966, Chapter Two.

beginning of the Christian era—most suggested dates are still extremely rough and tentative—iron-working had become widespread, trade across the Sahara was going on with some regularity, and many states had begun to develop centralized political institutions under rulers who received divine honors and were credited with divine attributes.

There are disagreements as to whence the stimulus for all these changes came. Some British writers have emphasized influences from the northeast, especially from the kingdom of Kush—itself the heir to much of the legacy of ancient Egypt—whose capital of Meröe was a center of iron-working which has been compared to Birmingham, England. Relatively small aristocratic groups, they suggest, may have entered West Africa as warriors or conquerors, bringing with them the new technology and perhaps also the new political concepts. This view may be supported by the persistence with which African peoples in their traditional histories claim Egyptian or Yemenite origins, although we must not think of these as necessarily implying mass migrations across Africa, but as reflecting the influence which an aristocratic minority may impose upon the historical consciousness of a people. (An extreme form of "northeastern" view is to be found in the works of a Senegalese writer, Cheikh Anta Diop, who claims that the Egyptian Pharaohs were themselves Negroes and that the Wolofs of modern Senegal are their lineal descendants.) Other writers believe that a more important source of influence upon the Western Sudan may have been Morocco and the western parts of North Africa; they claim that there is more reliable evidence of actual use of the ancient trade routes across the Sahara than of those through Wadai or Darfur. These views are of course not mutually exclusive; some regions may have been more influenced from the Nile valley, others from the northwest. In any case the most serious danger of distortion seems to lie in the uncritical acceptance of "diffusionist" theories of historical development which imply that some such external influence must necessarily be decisive. It seems wiser to keep an open mind about the influence exerted by these hypothetical invaders, and to assume that in the prehistoric and protohistoric periods the societies of West Africa were evolving in their own right as they came to terms with the problems of the environment. Whoever the first inhabitants of the Western Sudan may have been, they seem to have been capable of absorbing many successive streams of foreign influence and using them in the development of institutions and cultures, which can only be described as Sudanic, or simply African.

These debates apart, it remains clear that the trans-Saharan trade represented a continuing channel of external influence on the Western Sudan. The Sahara desert is often thought as essentially a barrier between Mediterranean and tropical Africa, because, before the advent of modern technology, it was difficult and dangerous to cross. So was the Atlantic Ocean; yet historians, as well as contemporary statesmen, find it useful to think of something called "the Atlantic community." For comparable reasons, there has recently been a growing tendency to abandon the concept of a distinct cultural entity called "Africa south of the Sahara."

Archaeologists are still extending and modifying our views of the historical significance of trans-Saharan contacts. The evidence of such rock-paintings as the famous Tassili frescoes, suggesting that there were once substantial populations of dark- as well as light-skinned people in what is now waterless desert, refers to a distant period, perhaps five thousand years ago, when the riverbeds which are traceable in many parts of the desert still ran with water. A major desiccation due to climatic change took place somewhere around the period when the Pharaohs were establishing their rule in Egypt; hence throughout historic times travellers have had to navigate with extreme care between the dispersed oases where water and dates are to be found. Herodotus gives a circumstantially convincing account of a crossing of the desert by five young men from Cyrene, but this seems to have been something exceptional; Roman military expeditions penetrated quite deeply into the desert, certainly to Fezzan, but they probably never crossed it.

Yet trade of some sort was already going on. Two Roman coins have been found in Mauritania, near long-established caravan routes; and paintings of wheeled chariots such as Herodotus says were used by the Garamantes of Fezzan have been found along both this route and a more easterly one which runs from Libya through Hoggar toward Gao. It is quite conceivable that such vehicles should have been drawn across the desert by oxen which had become adapted to life in a waterless environment; there are still breeds of African cattle capable of travelling without water for eight days. But during the first four centuries after Christ, there was introduced to North Africa the camel, which can travel ten or more days without water, and at a higher speed than most oxen. The consequent extension of the range of desert transport permitted trans-Saharan trade to develop on a more solidly organized basis.

Before the tenth century camels were regularly traversing, not only the two ancient cart routes already mentioned, but others which linked the major trading centers of North Africa with new markets developing in the Sudan, through desert oases controlled by formidable tribes of Berber nomads. The actual conduct and financing of the trade at its southern end seems to have been largely controlled by wealthy Arabo-Berber merchants resident in the caravan ports. The oldest constituent of the southward trade was salt, scarce and precious in the tropical savanna, chiefly collected from desert salt-pans like Taghaza. From the shores of the Mediterranean, horses, beads, copper, swords, paper, and luxury textiles reached the Sudan in growing quantities. Northwards went a little ivory (the North African elephants were by now almost hunted out), a few thousand slaves a year,[1] and above all, gold. From the time when the Arabs began to develop this trade in the eighth century until the discovery of America, West Africa provided the principal source of gold for Europe and the Arab world.

The most accessible gold deposits (known collectively as Wangara) were those of Bambouk in the upper Senegal valley and Bouré on the upper Niger; some supplies may have come from as far afield as Ashanti. The gold was brought to market centers on the southern borders of the desert by Mande-speaking traders known as *dyulas*,[2] a group of people whose widely ranging activities have been of great and continuing importance in the cultural as well as the economic history of West Africa. The *sahel* country, as borderland between desert and savanna, became the area of major market centers of which Jenné probably had the longest continuous life. Here Moorish Berber or Arab merchants from the desert broke bulk, exchanging their goods

[1] M. Raymond Mauny thinks the medieval trade across the desert may have absorbed 20,000 slaves a year. This may be a little high; slaves seem to have been bought largely for domestic service or conspicuous display, and there was not that powerful economic motive to expand the market which was present in the later Atlantic trade. Africa too was only one source of supply for classical and medieval Mediterranean markets; highly valued slaves also came from northern and eastern Europe.

[2] The word *dyula*, which means "trader" in several Mande languages, is sometimes used as a general term for Sudanic traders (including, e.g., Sarakulé), but is also reserved for a specific Mandinka-speaking people.

for those of the *dyulas*. It was apparently around such towns that there grew up the earliest Sudanic monarchies which historians can identify.

It is not easy to say in what order these states were established, or to distinguish the ethnic origins of their early rulers. (Since there may have been a good deal of intermarriage, research designed to prove a "Berber" or "Negro" thesis is likely to prove unrewarding, and somewhat boring to those no longer sharing the nineteenth century concern about "purity of race.") The kingdom of Tekrur on the lower Senegal, in the district later known as Futa Toro, is thought by some to be as old as the Christian era; farther east, Sudanic monarchies can be identified in Kanem and around Gao before the ninth century. But the early monarchy of which most is known—and that which, because of its proximity to the gold deposits, was probably in its day the richest and strongest—is the one first identified by Al Fazari, an Arab astronomer of the eighth century, as "the territory of Ghana, the land of gold."

There survive only second-hand descriptions of ancient Ghana; the fullest was written in Spain about 1067 A.D. by a well-informed Arab, Al Bakri. But archaeological work at Kumbi Salleh, since 1914, has revealed the stone buildings of a city of up to 30,000 inhabitants, with features which tally rather well with these accounts. Ghana was evidently a divine monarchy, which exercised close control over the amount of gold released for commercial circulation, derived considerable revenue by taxation, and maintained a formidable army out of the proceeds. It is not certain whether the gold deposits actually lay within its territory, but Ghana's chief importance was clearly as a market center offering secure facilities for merchants, who would give and accept drafts on colleagues north of the Sahara for very considerable sums. In Al Bakri's time its kings were Negroes, probably Sarakulés, with customs broadly similar to those of modern animist peoples of West Africa; but many sources suggest that the state may have been founded by a light-skinned dynasty of Berbers, who were overthrown during the eighth century A.D. Ghana, in short, provides the first documented example of "Sudanic monarchy"; the appeal to contemporary Africans of its story is illustrated by the enthusiastic claims to consanguinity made by peoples of the English-speaking state, over five hundred miles away, which now bears its name.

Traditional histories of Ghana make it clear that its monarchy was established before the *hegira*—Muhammed's departure for Medina in 622 A.D. In 639 the expansion of Arab power into Egypt began; by the beginning of the eighth century the whole North African coastline was under the rule of Arabs who professed the new religion and enforced its precepts. Although some Berbers resisted its coming, others accepted Islam readily. Desert-dwellers like the earliest converts, they found its very austerity congenial; many Berber tribes adopted the puritanical teachings of the Kharijites, resisting the imposition of any human authority but accepting voluntarily the full rigor of Koranic discipline, and seeking to enforce it on reluctant neighbors. It need not imply a cynical view of human motives to point out that this call to make forcible converts by means of holy war has often been heard most insistently in those countries where the population has pressed hardest upon limited means of livelihood.

The holy wars of the Berbers in the centuries following their conversion form an important chapter in the history of the Maghreb. In the Sudan their major importance was in overthrowing the animist Sarakulé rulers of Ghana. When Al Bakri wrote, an austere Berber dynasty from Mauritania known as the Almoravids[3] had already begun a *jihad* in the western Sahara which eventually gave them, for a time, control of Morocco and southern Spain. About 1054 they seized control of Audoghast, an important caravan terminal held by Ghana since 990; in 1076 they launched a full-scale attack on Ghana, overthrew the dynasty, and forced many of its people to become orthodox Malikite Muslims. But this first attempt to create a theocratic state which would enforce the precepts of the Shari'a was short-lived, at least in the Sudan (it had a longer influence in Mauritania). The Almoravid ruler Abu Bakr was killed in 1087, and for more than a century the Sarakulé of Ghana recovered their independence, though apparently with diminishing power.

In fact, until the eighteenth century Islam advanced more effectively in the Western Sudan through the influence of traders on their countries of residence than through the power of warriors. In Gao, King Kossoi accepted the new religion about 1009 as a result of the

---

[3] From *al-murabitum*, the men of the *ribat*, or convent, since their original base was a religious community on an island in the Senegal river. The term *marabout* is commonly used for Muslim clerics in French-speaking West Africa; more exactly, it denotes religious leaders practicing the cult of saints, especially in Mauritania, Senegal, and Mali.

argument of Muslim merchants from the north; Tekrur is said to have been converted by a king who died in 1040-1. And indeed in Ghana itself Islam was making peaceful progress before the Almoravid conquest. Al Bakri describes the Muslims as inhabiting a separate town, with twelve mosques; but even in the king's town there were many signs of Muslim influence. "The king's interpreters, the controller of his treasury, and the majority of his viziers are chosen from among the Muslims," Al Bakri wrote. Clearly there were intrinsic attractions in the new religion; to traders it offered a common bond to strengthen the goodwill of the northern merchants, to rulers a supply of learned men to serve the state, and a set of legal and political ideas which could be adapted to reinforce the basis of their own authority.

The acceptance of Islam among Negro peoples of the Sudan was thus a gradual process, not to be explained by any such simple formula as "the coming of the Arabs." Actual immigration by Arabs; their assimilation through conquest and intermarriage with certain of the Berber tribes, notably in Mauritania; the rise to religious authority of Arab families like the Kunta of Timbuktu; these were processes which extended over many centuries and culminated too late to have had a decisive influence on the states discussed in this chapter. In this first phase of Islamic expansion the crucial events were conversions of rulers; but these were generally voluntary and the converts did not necessarily accept rigid orthodoxy or seek to enforce canonical observances on reluctant subjects. These might therefore remain quite firmly attached to animistic beliefs or cults, and continue to profess ethical standards and modes of social behavior quite alien to the Shari'a. In the Sudan, even as more people became avowed Muslims, Islam came to absorb many syncretic features characteristic of indigenous African cultures; by embracing animistic practices, it may even have helped to ensure their survival.[4]

The growing points of Muslim influence were the towns—Gao, Timbuktu, Jenné, Kano—caravan ports or inland markets, where sizeable populations of craftsmen were weaving cotton, working in leather, iron, or gold, making pottery or basketwork with which to nourish the growing network of commerce still more strongly. The

[4] See especially Jean Rouch, *La Religion et la Magie chez les Songhai* (Paris, 1960).

development of urban wealth also provided new opportunities for state-building. After Ghana's decline, two major Muslim empires succeeded it in the general area of the middle Niger; their centers of power moved successively eastwards, perhaps reflecting shifts in the relative importance of the desert trade routes. Although these are not the only medieval Muslim states which may be considered as ancestors of the modern nations of French-speaking West Africa, it is to their memory that patriotic appeals are most frequently made.

The empire of Mali was founded by Mandinkas, a people whose conversion to Islam began in the eleventh century; in the thirteenth Sun-diata, possibly himself an animist, conquered Ghana, expanded his power into the southern Sahara and the lower valley of the Gambia, and controlled the actual goldfields of Bambouk and probably Bouré. The rulers of Mali thus held in their power more of the Sudan's wealth than Ghana had ever done; in 1324-5 Mansa Musa astonished the Muslim world by his rich entourage and his conspicuous expenditure when he visited Cairo on his pilgrimage to Mecca. A condition of this prosperity was the establishment of that security for travellers, traders, and their property throughout a wide area, which impressed Ibn Battuta when he visited Mali thirty years later. Yet much of the monarch's power depended on the control which he personally was able to establish over his provincial governors; later in the fourteenth century outlying peoples began to assert their independence. Among the first to break away were the Songhai of Gao; after 1464 Sonni Ali, a soldier and military organizer of genius made this town the center of a great empire, which left the Keita dynasty of Mali to a rapidly diminishing dominion in the upper Niger basin. Although some Muslim accounts of Ali's reign show a shrewd, cruel, powerful despot, whose irregular prayer life and tendencies to idol-worship shocked the *ulama*, a modern scholar regards him as a skillful statesman, balancing Islam against adherents of the traditional religion to further his control of this, the most extensive and powerful yet seen in the Sudan. Shortly after his death in 1492 a new dynasty was founded by a court official, Muhammed Askia, of a family said to have originated from Tekrur.[5] Adhering more closely to Malikite orthodoxy, and relying on the support of the

---

[5] See J. O. Hunwick, "Religion and State in the Songhai Empire, 1464-1591," in I. M. Lewis ed., *Islam in Tropical Africa* (London, 1966), pp. 296-315.

ulama, or learned Muslim community, he remodelled the administrative, fiscal, and military institutions of his state by methods which have been crudely compared to those of his contemporary, Henry VII of England.

Such comparisons with states of late medieval Europe must be accepted with reserve, pending more intensive study. The substantial volume of official records which has been preserved not only makes European states easier to study, but in itself suggests that their institutions were in many respects more sophisticated. The most effective rulers of Mali and Songhai clearly showed great political skill in mobilizing the wealth of their states to support impressive courts and formidable armies of mail-clad cavalry. But there are many vital questions about the way in which they were governed to which present evidence permits only partial or provisional answers. On what terms did the provincial and local representatives of central authority hold their positions? How were the taxes on trade, land, livestock, assessed and collected? Who made the laws, and how was justice administered? How far did the numerous officials of whose existence we know function with the cohesion and continuity of an effective bureaucracy? Until more scholarly research has been devoted to our fragmentary and often obscure authorities it is hard to go beyond the general impression that in these centuries there is no obvious or fundamental disparity between the power of the most effective West African rulers and that of their European contemporaries.

There is also room for debate about the position of Islam in these states. With the possible exception of Tekrur, they were not theocracies; their rulers did not have the means, nor perhaps the desire, to impose Muslim law and ritual at the expense of the varying beliefs and practices established by custom in the villages of their wide dominions. Under the Askiya, Islam might be described as the state religion of Songhai; Muhammed Askia's alliance with the clergy was cemented when on his pilgrimage of 1497-8 he was invested by the *Sherif* of Mecca with the Kalifate of Tekrur, meaning the Western Sudan. Under his predecessors, and under the rulers of Mali, some writers regard Islam as merely an "imperial cult." But it would be dangerous to assume that, because Muslim writers criticize the conduct and impugn the piety of men like Sonni Ali, Islamic influence in their states was negligible; nobody would draw parallel conclusions from the personal aberrations of rulers of medieval Christendom. Historians may reasonably accept professions of allegiance without going too deeply into moral balance sheets; there is clearly some sense at least in which both Mali and Songhai were Muslim states.

What did this mean for the life of society? For one thing, it provided incentives to make the *haj* or pilgrimage to Mecca, and so brought many thousands of Sudanese into contact with the wider Muslim world. In this period, the usual route seems to have been by way of Cairo, a great center of Islamic culture and learning; in 1342-3 a single party is said to have arrived with over five thousand pilgrims. This pilgrim traffic must have constituted a substantial part of the Sudan's external trade; in exchange for the gold, ivory, and slaves exported as travelling expenses, West Africa was importing *Hajis*. Few of her imports, until modern times at least, have been more admirable in their effects. Sudanese towns became centers in which the arts, crafts, and learning of the Muslim world were transmitted, and sometimes reinterpreted to suit Sudanese conditions. The Sankoré mosque at Timbuktu, attributed to the Spanish-born architect es-Saheli, illustrates how Islamic traditions were reinterpreted with African materials; it is an outstanding example of a distinctively Sudanic architectural style which can still be observed in modern Mali. In the towns at least *kadis* would administer Koranic law (though sometimes perhaps, only to foreign Muslims). In Jenné and Timbuktu learned Muslims not only taught their pupils to read the Koran, the commentaries, and other works of scholarship, and to write in Arabic script, but began to make their own contributions to Islamic jurisprudence. According to a famous description of early sixteenth-century Songhai by Leo Africanus,

> In Timbuktu there are numerous judges, doctors, and clerics, all receiving good salaries from the king. He pays great respect to men of learning. Many books in manuscript, imported from Barbary, are sold. More profit is made from this trade than from any other line of business.[6]

These books, doubtless mostly works of theology and jurisprudence, included classical Greek authors; in 1851 the traveller Barth dis-

[6] Jean-Léon l'Africain, *Description de l'Afrique*, A. Epaulard, trans. (Paris, 1956), II, 468-9.

covered manuscript translations of Plato and Aristotle in Baguirmi, south of Lake Chad. Euclid was known, and other works of mathematics and astronomy—sciences to which Islam contributed so much; doubtless also some historical chronicles, which inspired local scholars to follow suit. About 1519 a Negro Muslim, Mahmoud Kati, began to write the *Tarikh el Fettach*, the oldest known historical work actually produced in the Sudan.

But this learning, and the practices of the Muslim religion itself, penetrated beyond the urban communities only unevenly, and often in adulterated forms. Even among the rulers Koranic teaching was not always strictly observed or thoroughly known; Mansa Musa is said to have been genuinely surprised and upset to be told in Cairo that the sexual promiscuity he practiced was not lawful even for kings. Since the empires rarely accepted the obligation of enforcing conformity, the main agents of proselytization beyond the towns were for many centuries the *dyulas*. In many places, such as Kankan, these traders established distinct settlements, intermarrying with local women and conforming in many ways to local custom, while practicing the basic features of their religious discipline and building mosques where eventually they might be joined in prayer by the chiefs and people of the country. In such cases what emerged was a form of syncretism, where the people professed Islam without renouncing animistic beliefs, traditional laws and initiation rites, or respect for the practitioners of sorcery. In other areas itinerant *dyulas* commanded respect by virtue of their wealth, their literacy, their self-assurance and supposed supernatural powers; people who might not claim themselves to be Muslims would adapt Muslim practices in such matters as dress and the slaughter of animals, or buy scraps of the Koran as magical charms. Islamic influences thus became diffused very widely through the Sudan and into the forest belt, far beyond the borders of Muslim states themselves.

Some Sudanic peoples, however, resisted Islamization tenaciously and by force. Since all our documentary sources for this period were written by Muslims, it is difficult to identify all such cases. But the case of the Mossi-Dagomba group of states is particularly interesting, even though their early history is on many points obscure. Three of these—Wagadugu, Yatenga, Gurma—still exist as the nucleus of the Voltaic republic; two related states, Mamprussi and Dagomba, lie largely within modern Ghana. These Sudanic monarchies, united by

"mythical bonds of common descent and actual bonds of kinship," [7]
were established in roughly their present locations by mounted invaders from the northeast in the fourteenth or fifteenth centuries;
their intricately balanced political systems appear to have survived
with surprisingly little change until the French conquest. Their
cavalry repeatedly raided Timbuktu and the states of the Niger until
Muhammed Askia mobilized the force of *jihad* against them; even
then they defended the independence of their homelands with
tenacity and success. Muslim influences in Mossi society today are
not due to forcible conversions but to the peaceful influence which
Muslim settlers have brought to bear through its rulers since the
eighteenth century. The establishment and survival of the Mossi
states provides a warning against too simple an identification of this
medieval period of Sudanic history as one of Muslim ascendency.

Still, the Muslim empires represent one of the most impressive
achievements of African statecraft. Why was this achievement not
sustained? When the French and British occupied the Western
Sudan at the end of the nineteenth century, few of the medieval
empires had retained their political identity, and the states and
polities which had taken their place proved incapable of competing
technologically or militarily in a sustained encounter with European
states. There had been a relative decline of African strength, which
historians must try to explain.

It was a *relative* decline; the decisive point was the expansion of
Europe, not the atrophy of Africa. This is no place to review the
familiar problems concerning the growth of trade and accumulation
of capital in certain European countries; the development in western
Europe of modern scientific methods; the rise of new technologies
and the take-off of successive Western countries into self-sustaining
economic growth. The relevant point is that nothing comparable
took place in that medieval Muslim civilization of which the Sudanic
empires formed a part. Arab achievements in medicine and mathematics were followed up in Christian Europe, while the dominant
intellectual interests of Islam became sterile stamping grounds of
theological legalism. At the same time, the principal growing-point
of the commerce and wealth of the world were moving from the
Mediterranean basin to the north Atlantic seaboards.

[7] Elliott P. Skinner, *The Mossi of the Upper Volta* (Stanford, 1964) p. 138.
This anthropological study has much to teach historians of West Africa.

This economic change had effects in Africa, which will be discussed in the next chapter. As Europeans found their way down the coastline, West Africa's foreign trade became oriented toward the ocean, and in time came to consist principally of the export of slave labor. But the direct consequences of this for the Western Sudan should not be exaggerated. Except in the lower Senegal and Gambia valleys, the catchment areas of oceanic and desert trade remained largely distinct, at least until the eighteenth century; the bulk of the slaves sent to America were from the coastal forests, rather than the Sudanese states. There is little evidence that the Western Sudan suffered either severe depopulation or loss of earnings as a result of the Atlantic slave trade.

However, some of the gold of Ashanti, Bouré and Bambouk which had previously crossed the Sahara was in the sixteenth century being sent instead to the coast. This meant loss of revenue to Songhai—and also to the rulers of the Maghreb. Sultan Ahmed el-Mansur of Morocco, after defeating the Portuguese invasion at el-Ksar in 1578, began to seek direct control of the gold of the Sudan and the salt of the Sahara. In 1591 a well-disciplined Moroccan army of perhaps 4,000, including many European Muslims, somehow accomplished the crossing of the desert, routed the Songhai army near Gao by its use of firearms, sent back consignments of gold and other loot, and established a Moroccan *pashalik* at Timbuktu. This government never proved as effective as the regime it had destroyed. By 1660 the *pashas* ceased to answer even nominally to Moroccan control (though Timbuktu retained sentimental and cultural ties with Fez until the end of the nineteenth century). As the settlers with whom Morocco had hoped to colonize the Sudan began to quarrel among themselves, former subjects of Songhai—Bambaras and Fulas along the Niger, Tuareg and other Berber nomads from the desert—seized the opportunity to assert their independence. The author of the *Tarikh-es-Sudan* bewailed the atrophy of political order.

Security has given place to danger, prosperity to misery and calamity, whilst affliction and distress have succeeded well being. Over the length and breadth of the land the people began devouring one another, raiding and war sparing neither wealth nor status, disorder spreading and intensifying until it became universal.

The Sultan of Morocco, by virtue of his sherifian descent, continued to command what an eighteenth-century observer called "a transitory respect" [8] among Muslims in Mauritania and some northern parts of the Sudan; Friday prayer might be offered in his name, and individual Moroccans might enjoy a certain reflected prestige. But the Sultan lacked power to control events anywhere in the Sudan.

Political disintegration was accompanied by a decline in the influence of Islam. Peoples who had not previously asserted their identity founded new states, practicing animist religious rites, administering customary laws which often showed only pale traces of Muslim practice. Outstanding examples are the two Bambara kingdoms of Ségou and Kaarta, founded by the Koulibali and Massassi clans in the seventeenth and eighteenth centuries respectively; while initially they tolerated and respected Muslim traders and clerics, and even adopted some of their teachings, these Bambaras were to resist fiercely attempts to impose Muslim theocratic rule in the nineteenth century. But that resistance belongs to a different chapter in the history of West African Islam.

[8] Matra (British Consul in Morocco) to Banks, March 28, 1789 (R. Hallett, *Records of the African Association*, London, 1964, p. 81). See also P. Labarthe, *Voyage au Sénégal* (Paris, An X.) p. 35.

THREE

The Forest and the Ocean

The early history of the forest belt presents even more serious problems than that of the Western Sudan. There are no written accounts earlier than the fifteenth century. Physical and climatic conditions make archaeology difficult, and only in certain districts has important work yet been done. Students of the early history of the forest peoples thus have to rely heavily on orally transmitted evidence, supplemented by ethnographic and philological observations; few chronological checks can be imposed on this material before the period when Europeans learned to sail down the African coast and to describe what they found. But these travellers often had difficulty in understanding the perplexingly unfamiliar communities they visited and their accounts are in any case limited to certain portions of the seaboard.

The general purport of this early evidence suggests that the forest was once a place of refuge for peoples migrating from the Sudan, perhaps in consequence of major political or religious upheavals there. In the safety of the forest, where cavalry could not follow them, these refugees became dispersed, sometimes settling in communities which represented little more than a single extended family. Some of the forest peoples which today retain an identifiable language or "tribal" identity may originally have represented little more than a cluster of such extended families or village settlements. Yet this fragmentation must not be equated with anarchy. Small states are not necessarily disorderly or unstable; even the puzzled and fragmentary comments of early European travellers show that many such peoples had succeeded in stabilizing relations with their neighbors over quite wide areas. The sixteenth-century Portuguese writer Alvares d'Almada, identifying eight different peoples on the coasts of modern Guinea and Sierra Leone, grouped them together under the general

name of the "Sapes nations": he felt able to give a general account
of their political structure and customs, and added "all these understand one another." Here as in other areas secret "country societies,"
associations whose functions and powers are not fully understood
by outsiders even today, contributed to political stability. Although
the primary role of such societies seems usually to be the education
of young men or women in preparation for adult life within their
community, some at least assumed wider responsibilities for regulating
social behavior. The Dutch geographer Dapper described how the
Poro could enforce its prohibitions in the seventeenth century; more
than two hundred years later recognizably similar methods were used
to boycott the export of palm produce. Membership of this society
provided an underlying unity which transcended the boundaries of
apparently independent chiefdoms, and still transcends the modern
boundaries of Guinea, Liberia, and Sierra Leone.

Elsewhere in the forests, very different societies developed: powerful
states with sizeable towns and high material cultures, especially
notable for their achievements in the plastic arts. The outstanding
examples of these, Ife and Benin, lie within the boundaries of modern
Nigeria; but the Aja peoples who formed states in southern Dahomey
and Togo during the seventeenth century shared much of their
political and cultural tradition. In the Ivory Coast, somewhat later,
sizeable states were founded by the Baoulé and the Agni, Akan
peoples related to the Ashanti. Political unity in the forest had to be
expressed through institutions equally unfamiliar to Europeans and
to African Muslims. A Yoruba historian argues that both Aja and
Yoruba rulers "regarded the state as a larger version of the family";
while administering their affairs independently they continued to
acknowledge the paternal seniority of one state—Ife among the
Yoruba, Allada among the Aja—as custodian of the traditions of
this vastly extended family. "Common culture, common religious
beliefs, common currency and a common language . . . flowed from
this original source." [1]

The cultural history of the forest peoples must largely be studied
by inference from the life of their modern descendants—a method of

[1] Isaac A. Akinjogbin, *Dahomey and its Neighbours, 1708-1818* (Ph.D. thesis,
University of London, 1963), pp. 9-10. I am grateful to Dr. Akinjogbin for permission to quote from this work, shortly to be published by the Cambridge University Press.

reasoning to be used with caution. But although, among the French-speaking peoples of today, only those of southern Dahomey can authenticate sculptural traditions as old as those of Ife, there is clearly no reason to suppose that those who made images in durable materials were the only Africans whose culture looked beyond the material needs of existence. Among many non-Muslim peoples traditions of representational woodcarving, usually associated with religious needs—the representation of protecting spirits or the provision of masks for ritual dance—appear to be long established; they are particularly rich among the modern Baoulé (and in the Sudan, among the Bambara and the Dogon.) Rhythmic music and dance, too, have for many centuries been integral parts of African social activity, associated with work and worship, recreation and war. Early visitors to both coast and savanna describe horns, stringed instruments, and percussion very similar to those still in use today, and Leo Africanus provides an agreeable glimpse of a Negro orchestra performing in the cosmopolitan city of Fez.

Clearly there was, as there is still, great variety in the ways of life of the forest people. Those settled in the more remote and unproductive areas doubtless led a very simple existence, supported largely by hunting and gathering forest produce; but in areas where conditions permitted denser settlement agricultural methods might be skillfully related to the environments. Some peoples practiced mixed farming. Coastal dwellers developed fisheries, in boats crudely but skillfully fashioned from tree trunks. And much of the area was kept in contact with the Sudanese kingdoms by the ubiquitous *dyulas*, who penetrated deep into the forest and as far as the coasts of the Gulf of Guinea. The attraction of trade with the area of Ashanti lay not only in its gold but in its kola nuts, a refreshing stimulant and food much valued by desert travellers, and by Muslims who took the prohibition of alcohol seriously. In return *dyulas* brought to the forest-dwellers salt, beads, cloth—and also contact with Sudanic cultures. Sometimes they settled to form discrete communities in important market centers like Kankan, Kong, and Bobo-Dioulasso, which then became bases for trade still further afield; sometimes animist rulers employed them as advisers or clerks. But everywhere *dyulas* were united, for their temporal advantage and spiritual welfare, in the brotherhood of Islam. Even if they did not seek converts their superior learning and sophistication and the prestige of their Koranic schools commanded respect, and sometimes the flattery of imitation.

Before the sixteenth century, forest-dwellers can have had few other contacts with horizons wider than those of their immediate neighbors. The basic social structure would normally comprise chiefly families and other notables, free cultivators, hunters or fishermen, and household slaves. Such specialized careers as were offered by the practice of handicrafts were often, as in Senegambia, the preserve of endogamous hereditary "castes" of weavers, leather-workers, or smiths (whose wives might enjoy a monopoly of pottery-making) and other tradesmen. A closed group with no exact parallel elsewhere was that of the *griots* (somewhat inadequately translated as "minstrels"), on whom there fell in preliterate societies the responsibility for conserving traditions. Although often feared and despised (so that early travellers in Senegambia equated their position with that of European Jews) some *griots* were retained as praise-singers or official chroniclers to chiefs and notable families; others enjoyed a certain independence, even a position as social critics or satirists. But to see the *griots* as providing traditional African society with the equivalent of a free press would be anachronistic; for what could social criticism achieve, so long as the possibilities of change seemed ineluctably limited? There is more than one sense in which the modern history of the forest belt may legitimately be dated from the first contacts with Europe.

First Trading Contacts with Europe

The first authenticated voyage by a European beyond Cape Bojador (now in Spanish Sahara) was made by the Portuguese Gil Eannes in 1434. (The story of fourteenth-century voyages from Dieppe to the Gulf of Guinea, first advanced in 1669, was discredited by the French historian de la Roncière in 1912; and M. Mauny has since argued that navigational conditions must in any case have precluded the return journey up the west coast until Portuguese seamen of the fifteenth century learned the secret of sailing westward in order to sail north. It is possible however that Carthaginians made the journey by galley.) Once Portuguese caravels had broken this navigational barrier, exploration of the African coast proceeded in successive stages, encouraged by a dynasty unusually sensitive to the problems of maritime enterprise. Cape Verde was reached in 1444, the Gold Coast in

1471, the Congo mouth in 1483. Thereafter Portugal's maritime frontier moved on toward the Cape of Good Hope, and the incalculable riches of the Indian Ocean trade. On the West African coast the Portuguese left behind a sparse chain of forts and trading settlements, where they struggled to maintain the monopoly they claimed against growing pressure from foreign interlopers, Castilians and Flemings in the fifteenth century, French, English, and Dutch in the sixteenth. The Portuguese built a fort at Arguin, off the Mauritanian coast, in 1448: founded an entrepôt in the Cape Verde Islands, which became the base from which many Portuguese or Eurafrican traders settled on the coasts of modern Senegal and Guinea; built the first of the mainland forts of the Gold Coast at Elmina in 1482; and from the end of the fifteenth century encouraged settlement on the island of San Thomé. These were the first of many toe-holds on and off the African littoral from which Europeans for many centuries sought to confound their enemies, develop trade with the African peoples, and sometimes, even, transmit to Africa something of the beliefs and culture of the Christian civilization which they claimed to represent.

Hopes of commerce, which might strengthen Christian monarchs against the Muslim Arabs and against one another, had brought Europeans to West Africa. Commerce would shape their future relationships there. But what produce had the coastal peoples to offer that could support the heavy overhead costs of regular oceanic trade? They could offer provisions to merchantmen sailing east; some ivory, according to the fortunes of the hunt; Malaguetta pepper, a valued luxury in which the Portuguese monarchy struggled to maintain a Royal monopoly. Initially it was gold which provided the strongest attraction; if West African supplies could be diverted from the Saharan route to the ocean, Christian Portugal would be greatly strengthened against the North African Muslims. Arguin, at first, seemed to offer hopes of achieving this; caravans were attracted away from the Saharan route, and for a time in the 1480s the Portuguese King found it worthwhile to maintain an agent at an inland market called Wadan. John II also tried unsuccessfully to create a client state among the Wolof, and he and his successors sent missions (of which relatively little is known) to negotiate about trade with the ruler of Mali. But by this time the center of power in the Sudan was already moving eastward, to Songhai; moreover the relative importance of the Sudanese gold supply was also declining. Ashanti miners were supplying the forts of the Gold Coast, but even so America was dwarfing Africa as a source of bullion. Europeans continued to buy gold on the Senegal and Guinea coasts as long as opportunities offered; but here as elsewhere, it was slaves that came to dominate West Africa's trade with Europe.

Such works as Azurara's *Chronicle of the Discovery and Conquest of Guinea* are full of accounts of slave raids carried out by the earliest travellers on the coasts of Mauritania and Senegal. Initially the aim was to obtain information or recruit interpreters for future voyages; by midcentury it became apparent that captives could be profitably sold for domestic service or general labor in Europe, and that a greater supply could be obtained, more easily, by barter with Moorish and Negro authorities than by violent raids. By 1455 Cadamosto estimated the export of slaves from Arguin alone (perhaps generously) at one thousand a year; it was beginning to overshadow the gold trade for which the fort had been established. Soon the sugar plantations of San Thomé provided another market for slaves bought by the Portuguese in the Bight of Benin; others again were traded for gold at Elmina until King John III, "ever more mindful of the salvation of souls than of the profits of his treasury," ordered that slaves should be sold only in Christian markets. Later, the French monarchy recruited African slaves to man its galleys in the Mediterranean.

Modern readers may find the note of high religious concern which colors such early Portuguese references to the slave traffic sanctimoniously repulsive. Yet at this period Christians and Muslims alike saw in enslavement of infidels an opening of the doors of salvation, rather than a breach of moral law. In Mauritania and Senegal, if not necessarily on more southerly coasts, the demands of the Saharan trade seem already to have legitimized the practice of selling certain sorts of person out of the community: prisoners of war certainly, perhaps also debtors, witches, and felons. Although the raids of the early travellers may temporarily have introduced a new element of violence, the immediate effects of Europe's entry into the commercial slave markets of these areas must have been principally to increase demand, raise prices, and so perhaps to encourage African slave brokers to seek new sources of supply. Only by degrees did the scale of demand increase so drastically as to involve a total transformation in the life of some of the coastal peoples.

The cause of this change was the growing demand for African labor on colonial plantations in the Americas, and the development of large scale commercial organization in Europe to meet it. Spaniards seem to have begun using Negro slaves on West India sugar plantations early in the sixteenth century, and the Portuguese soon developed their own plantations in Brazil; but it was only after 1640, when sugar was introduced to islands settled by French and English colonists, that the Atlantic slave trade became an essential part of one of the most rapidly expanding sectors of the European commercial economy. As the transatlantic labor market grew, European slaveships clustered along the African coast, and African entrepreneurs responded by seeking new ways to meet their apparently insatiable demands. Estimates of the numbers involved are still little more than broad approximations; those commonly accepted as the most judicious available suggest 900,000 as the number of slaves landed in the Americas in the sixteenth century and 2,750,000 for the seventeenth. For the eighteenth century, when the famous "triangular trade" played such an important part in European mercantilist rivalries, the estimate is seven million, with another four million landed during the first two-thirds of the nineteenth century, when the demands of cotton plantations in the U.S.A. and new sugar plantations in Cuba and Brazil outweighed the effects of the growing campaign to prohibit the trade.[2] But when considering the effects on Africa, allowances must also be made for slaves who died during the process of collecting cargoes in Africa (e.g., on marches to the coast) or during the terrible "middle passage" across the Atlantic. On any single voyage all slaves might survive or all might die, depending partly on the preparations made by the captain, partly on random medical factors; an average figure for deaths on the voyage may be somewhere around one in eight. It is not possible to translate these estimates into calculations of demographic loss, for we do not know the exact limits of the area from which slaves were regularly drawn for the Atlantic market, nor its population in this period. But it seems clear that many of the coastal districts between Mauritania and southern Angola suffered population losses more serious than those of the Sudanic countries which supplied the trans-Saharan trade, and

[2] Figures cited in John D. Fage, An Introduction to the History of West Africa (Cambridge, 1955), pp. 82-3.

that the slave traffic in one way or another dominated the early contacts with Europe of most of their peoples.

The Slave Trade in Mauritania and Senegal

Although by the eighteenth century no part of the West African coast remained wholly unaffected by slave-dealing, there were big variations in the scale of the trade, the methods employed, and the effects on African society. On the barren coasts of Mauritania and in the *sahel* country south of the Senegal estuary, Moorish and Wolof states on the whole remained strong enough to retain considerable control over the conduct of trade, while the conditions in which enslavement was legitimate were in some degree controlled by Koranic law and precept. In the nineteenth as in the fifteenth century many of the slaves sold in the Senegal and near Cape Verde seem to have been brought by caravan traders from at least as far inland as Bambara country, and might otherwise have been sent across the old Saharan route. Such figures as exist do not suggest that this area ever experienced a really heavy drain on its population.

Foreign commerce may however have accelerated the break-up of the Wolof empire, which in the fifteenth century extended from the Senegal to the Gambia river, comprehending the territories now known as Joloff, Cayor, Baol, Walo, Sine, and Saloum. About 1488 Bemoy, a claimant to this empire who had responded skillfully to the opportunities of trade with Portugal, found his title challenged in arms by his half-brothers; it seems impossible to say whether this was because of something he had done in the course of business, or simply represented a dynastic dispute. He sought the aid of John II of Portugal; when this was made conditional upon baptism, this ruler of a largely Muslim empire travelled to Lisbon, was received with public ceremonial and religious instruction, and declared his conversion to the Christian faith. He then returned to the Senegal with an escort of twenty caravels and a Portuguese working-party who were to build a fort at the mouth of the river as a base for trade with Timbuktu, where the Portuguese believed they would find "the richest trades and markets of gold in the world." [3] But Bemoy quarrelled with his Portuguese escort and was killed; the empire, far

---

[3] Pina, *Chronica del Rey Dom Joao II*, trans. J. W. Blake, *Europeans in West Africa, 1450-1560* (London: Hakluyt Society, 1942), I, 85.

from providing a field for peaceful Portuguese penetration, began to disintegrate. Impressed by this demonstration of Portuguese power Wolof notables, in the words of the chronicler Barros, "all began to do their best to despatch the King's trading ships . . . and to send presents and promises, in their own interests and in the hope of obtaining similar help from him should they need it, or from fear of angering him." [4] Wars among the Wolof continued and imported firearms were increasingly used; prisoners were sold as slaves on an increasing scale; Sine and Saloum established their independence.[5] By midcentury Cayor, Baol, and Walo had followed suit; conflict among these succession states became a normal feature of Senegambian politics, even though revolted vassals might continue to show signs of deference and respect to the Bourba Joloff. An early concern of such states was to establish ports for regular trade with Europeans, which provided ready markets for their prisoners of war.

Senegal was thus among the first regions of Africa to be drawn into the Atlantic slave economy; it was also the first to receive a permanent French settlement. By the eighteenth century trade in the river was controlled by a powerful commercial company, which had subjected its dealings in human beings to the obscenity of bureaucratic definition; units of exchange were here defined in the notional currency of "pieces of India." Four children aged 8 to 14, or six aged 4 to 8, counted as three pieces of India, or the equivalent of three healthy adults; robust males under 30 who had lost an eye or a few fingers were marked down by half; blind or epileptic or consumptive slaves were not recognized as legal tender at all, but elephantiasis or missing teeth did not make a human being unnegotiable. Here as elsewhere on the coast the market in men had become fully commercialized.[6]

Yet the French India Company, which controlled the Senegal trade, did not find its business in slaves sufficiently large to justify the cost of regular transatlantic voyages. Even at the height of the Atlantic slave trade it seems to have been unusual for the Senegal

[4] Joao de Barros, *Asia*, trans. G. R. Crone, *The Voyages of Cadamosto and other Documents* (London: Hakluyt Society, 1937), p. 142.
[5] V. Fernandes, *Description de la Côte Occidentale d'Afrique*, ed. T. Monod, A. Texeira da Mota, R. Mauny (Bissau, 1951), pp. 19, 28-31.
[6] Treaty between the Compagnie des Indes and the Guinea consortium of Nantes, October 16, 1750. André Delcourt, *La France et les Etablissements français au Sénégal entre 1731 et 1763* (Dakar, 1952), pp. 413-8.

region to export more than one thousand slaves a year. Moreover, though some were prisoners taken in the Wolof wars, the majority seem to have been Bambaras, brought from countries in modern Mali for sale at French trading posts further up the river. Even allowing for further sales of Bambaras and Mandinkas to British traders in the Gambia, the Atlantic trade seems to have constituted a relatively moderate drain on the populations of modern Senegal and Mauritania. By the eighteenth century Senegambia was developing a more diversified export trade which involved exceptional patterns of Afro-European relations.

The Rivers of Guinea

The rivers which intersect the coast of modern Guinea were first opened to oceanic trade by Portuguese merchants operating under royal monopoly out of the Cape Verde Islands (where as early as 1470 there was a settled Portuguese colony with its own church). They quickly built up chains of resident agents and factors along the navigable waterways south of Cape Verde: these expatriate Portuguese accepted African authority, married African women, and so founded settled communities of Christian Eurafricans whose growing influence provided some of the earliest, tenuous, channels for cultural contact between Europe and Africa. One of the main trading centers on this coast was Cacheo; here Fernandes describes weekly markets, held under the supervision of the chief and his *cadis*, which he generously estimates to have attracted 8,000 people from up to 60 miles around.

Until the nineteenth century the French and Portuguese did more trade in the Casamance and the rivers which now form part of Portuguese Guinea than in those farther south (in part because strong Muslim influence, and the contacts with the hinterland which it brought, date only from the Futa Jalon *jihad* of 1725). The Nunez at least was exporting ivory and slaves from the sixteenth century onward, but there are relatively few accounts of its trade. By the later eighteenth century resident brokers, Africans or Eurafricans of Portuguese descent, seem to have collected the exports and shipped them in locally-built coasting craft for export from the Sierra Leone area; English traders were also taking advantage of relatively mild climate and good water supply in the Isles de Los to establish trading factories there. But the shortage of documents makes it difficult to assess the effects of this trade on Guinean society. Doubtless

European adventurers sometimes troubled the area for profit; Alvares d'Almada describes how the "Manes" (invaders from the interior in the midsixteenth century who have been identified with the modern Vai), were assisted by a Portuguese warrior with three muskets. But this technical military assistance did not save the Manes from defeat by an alliance of Susus and Fulas; in general the evidence does not suggest that the coming of trade very greatly increased political instability in the rivers or that the export of slaves reached such a scale as to cause severe depopulation or insecurity. The impression given by the few sources that we have for this period is of communities whose main activity remained subsistence agriculture, who controlled a modest trade in ivory, hides, and wax brought down from Futa Jalon and the near interior, and who also profited by selling off convicts and prisoners of war. After 1725 exports of slaves may have increased as a result of religious wars in Futa Jalon;[7] but this increase in supply seems to have taken place quite independently of foreign demand, and in any case to have been numbered in hundreds rather than thousands. Here as in Senegal, a moderate supply of slaves seems to have been drawn from quite a wide area. "As they trade very far inland," a French observer noted in 1779, "the Negroes that are found here, coming from a distance and in caravans, are tired out."[8]

The Ivory Coast

On most of the Ivory Coast—as Frenchmen began to call it in the eighteenth century—contacts between Africans and Europeans in the process of commerce was generally reduced to a minimum, for Europeans rarely attempted to live ashore. The usual procedure was for trading ships to signal their arrival by gunfire; African traders came out in canoes across the surf, and bargaining for ivory, slaves, or provisions took place on shipboard. Many Europeans distrusted the inhabitants of this coast; Barbot, for example, alleged of various peoples that they were cannibals with well-sharpened teeth, that they would sometimes kidnap European sailors, and that those at Cape Lahou "are apt to raise the price of ivory according to the number of ships

[7] See within, Ch. 4., p. 51.
[8] de Capellis, May 1779, quoted in J. Machat, Documents sur les Etablissements français de l'Afrique Occidentale au xviiie siècle (Paris, 1906), pp. 126-9.

they see off the coast." [9] This latter point suggests nothing more sinister than commercial acumen; and although cannibalism is known in the Ivory Coast, this was a charge often made indiscriminately during these early contacts, and by both sides. Africans too sometimes believed that Europeans bought slaves for use as food. The kidnappings represent African reprisals for the practice of certain disreputable Europeans of weighing anchor and enslaving chiefs or traders who had come aboard. But such irregular conduct was deplored by respectable merchants on both sides; and from the seventeenth to the nineteenth centuries a regular but fairly small scale offshore trade was maintained between the people of the Ivory Coast and Europeans. What is known of its nature suggests that it imposed a heavier drain on the elephant than on the human population of the region.

In the extreme east, however, the modern Ivory Coast overlaps territory formerly included in the term Gold Coast; and hopes of gold led Frenchmen to make one unsuccessful attempt to establish themselves ashore. In 1688 a French naval officer, Ducasse, visited the small coastal state of Assinie, left a small party of traders and a priest on shore, and took to France two hostages who were believed to be members of the Assinie royal family. (One of them, Aniaba, was baptized by the famous Bishop Bossuet; both were patronized by Louis XIV during their prolonged stay and granted commissions in a Royal regiment.) Although many Frenchmen were becoming anxious to increase their supply of slaves, it was gold from Ashanti that they hoped to reach through this new venture; there was even talk of importing slaves from Whydah to work the mines for the French.[10] But the project was a fiasco. The Assinians (who doubtless shared the French hope of ousting the Dutch and their African clients from part of the Ashanti trade) were bitterly disappointed when the War of the League of Augsburg prevented France from sending regular trading voyages (or even regular payments of rent). At last in 1701, a fort was built, and thirty Frenchmen, including two

[9] John Barbot, A Description of the Coasts of North and South Guinea, in Awnsham and John Churchill, A Collection of Voyages and Travels, Vol. V (London, 1732), pp. 139-44.
[10] Report by Damon, 1698, in Paul Roussier, L'Etablissement d'Issiny (Paris, 1935), pp. 76-7. This publication conveniently prints the main sources for this episode.

Dominican friars, were established there. The Africans were still eager to receive European mechandise (putting muskets and powder at the top of their list); when a French officer inquired about future possibilities of trading in slaves they pressed him to buy eleven who happened to be surplus in their hands.[11] But again a European war interrupted trade, and this time it brought a Dutch attack on Assinie in November 1702. The Assinians lost confidence in their French protectors; a few months later the remaining Frenchmen retreated in the face of their hostility: Assinie remained untouched by foreign trade or influence, in any direct or important way, until the nineteenth century.

The Impact of the Slave Trade on Dahomey

Three of the four stretches of coastline eventually incorporated in French West Africa were thus touched relatively lightly by the slave trade; but among the Aja peoples of modern Dahomey its effects were profound. During the later seventeenth century they explored the possibilities of trading with Europeans and found them interested above all in buying slaves. The country between the Volta river and the Lagos lagoon became known to Europeans as the Slave Coast "because the whole trade there consists in slaves and gold, purchased merely by chance and in an inconsiderable quantity." [12] Various Aja states, of which Allada was the senior, organized this trade with much skill. Whydah alone exported between ten and fifteen thousand a year, and English, French, Dutch, Portuguese, and Brandenburg traders all at various times had permanent establishments there. According to the Dutch writer Bosman, Europeans gave extensive credit to African middlemen who would travel up to two hundred miles to inland slave markets. This relatively densely-populated region could supply slaves in sufficiently large numbers to justify foreign merchants in paying quite heavy customs duties ("100 pounds in Guinea value") in return for the ordered market facilities which the rulers of Whydah provided. But, precisely because of the importance of these supplies in the Atlantic economy, the various Europeans also began to intervene in African politics, backing one state in war against another in attempts to secure favorable conditions

---

[11] *Ibid.*, p. 104—Damon, 1702.
[12] Barbot, *loc. cit.*, p. 319.

for their own nation. The Aja responded by showing less regard for kinship and tradition, more for considerations of profit and power politics. After 1708 Whydah ceased to show the filial deference formerly due to Allada, now its great commercial rival. Meanwhile, further north, a new and strongly centralized monarchy was growing up around Abomey, founded apparently by Fon refugees from Allada who wished to escape from slave raiders, and other manifestations of the change in Aja society.

This new state, Dahomey, became the cuckoo of the now quarrelsome Aja breed. In 1724 and 1727 Agaja, the able and vigorous ruler of Abomey (1708-40), conquered in turn Allada and Whydah, and so acquired a coastline. Eighteenth-century writers, Snelgrave, Norris, and Dalzel, interpreted this as a drive for direct participation in the slave trade and its profits, as well as for direct access to supplies of fire-arms. Recent research by the Nigerian historian I. A. Akinjogbin suggests that Agaja's intentions were firstly to assert a dynastic claim to constitutional precedence among the Aja family of peoples, and secondly to put an end to systematic slave-trading as injurious to his own subjects.[18] But after 1730 Agaja turned reluctantly to slaving himself, having discovered that only by selling men could he obtain the guns and other trade goods which he needed to compete with his neighbors in power and prestige. Allada had of recent years paid tribute to the powerful Yoruba kingdom of Oyo, with which Dahomey found itself embroiled after 1726 and whose overlordship they were forced to acknowledge until 1818.

Dahomey, already a strongly centralized state, now developed despotic institutions of a sort unusual in West Africa as it struggled to maintain independence of action against Yorubas, Europeans, and other enemies, including refugees from Whydah. The state capital remained inland at Abomey; to excuse the kings from coming within range of European naval artillery, a quasireligious "tradition" de-

---

[18] I. A. Akinjogbin, "Agaja and the Conquest of the Coastal Aja States, 1724-30," *Journal Historical Society of Nigeria*, II (1963), 545-66. For a contemporary statement of a similar view cf. John Atkins, A Voyage to Guinea (London, 1735), pp. 119-22. Atkins draws much of his evidence from a disgruntled slave-trader (William Snelgrave, An Account of Some Parts of Guinea, London, 1734), whose own view of Agaja is less idealistic than Atkins'; he admits, however, that Agaja "drives no regular Trade in Slaves, but only sells such as he takes in his Wars" (p. 125).

veloped which forbade them to look on the sea.[14] Yet seaborne trade
was now essential to the Dahomean state, as testified by the presence
of a bas-relief of a two-masted caravel among the royal regalia. Agaja
closed the ports of Allada and centralized his foreign commerce at
Whydah under the political control of a royal official known as the
Yavogan. The slave trade continued, not simply because of the influence of African entrepreneurs, but as a means of fortifying the
Dahomean monarchy. (Hence the anomaly of the apparently wasteful "customs," where substantial numbers of saleable prisoners were
ceremonially executed each year; these had the effect both of discharging the religious duties of the king toward his ancestors and of
providing a terrible reminder of his earthly power.) The kings needed
flintlocks and powder for their armies, and sought to monopolize
their import; but arms could only be obtained by supplying slaves to
Europeans at competitive prices. Unfortunately supplies of slaves
might fluctuate according to the number of prisoners taken in war;
demand also was liable to fall off when Europeans became involved
in their own inter-tribal wars, and the Dahomean monopoly was
breached by the growth of rival trading centers in neighboring countries: the small principalities known as the Popos in the west, and
in the east Badagry, and the growing Aja state of Ajase Ipo, or Porto
Novo. To attract Europeans back again King Kpengla (1774-87)
resorted increasingly to slave raiding and military action against his
competitors. But his armies were not uniformly successful; his attempts to raise the price of slaves merely encouraged the Europeans
to move eastward to the well-supplied ports of the Niger delta; by
the end of the eighteenth century slave exports were reduced to
around three thousand a year, and no supplementary commerce had
been discovered. In Dahomey the demands of the slave traffic led
an African state into violent and ultimately self-defeating policies.

The Slave Trade in African History

Moralists may justly point out that turpitude becomes neither more
nor less deplorable when practiced on a large scale. It is pointless for
twentieth-century historians to deny that by their standards the trade,

[14] Similarly convenient "traditions" were cited to avoid direct contacts between
Europeans and rulers elsewhere in West Africa, including the *damel* of Cayor in
1870 [ANSOM, Sénégal I/56/b, Valière No. 334, 14 Aug. 1870]. Here the tradition originates after trade relations have been established; in 1455 Cadamosto
described his greeting by *Budomel* on the seashore (p. 35).

wherever practiced, involved cruel and inexcusable affronts to human dignity (though it should equally be recognized that many Africans and Europeans who engaged in it, acknowledged by their contemporaries as good men and citizens, sincerely believed that they were transgressing no binding principle of morality). This historian however does not believe that it is his task either to excuse atrocities by rationalization or to indulge in righteous indignation against those who committed sins to which his own generation is not tempted. Nor does it seem presently relevant to dwell on sufferings to which slaves were subjected after leaving African soil—the "horrors of the middle passage," the barbarities of plantation slavery in a commercial society—nor even to analyze the social and economic effects on the Americas of such a system. His immediate concern is to ascertain the effects of the slave trade on the peoples who remained in West Africa; and although this clearly varied locally, the problem raises certain general issues which have been fiercely debated ever since the morality and expediency of the trade were first questioned in Europe during the later eighteenth century.

Many writers, both African and European, see the commerce in slaves as the source of undiluted evil; like the Portugese earthquake of 1757, it can be made the universal excuse for all deficiencies, for every failure by Africans to equal the technological, economic, or political achievements of Europe. To M. Suret-Canale, it seems to have stifled and stunted African civilizations before they had reached their full development.[15] Other writers are less categorical; Mr. Christopher Wrigley believes that "the misfortune of most parts of eastern Africa was not that they had to endure the slave trade but that they had no trade at all." [16] Estimates of population loss which run into tens of millions are appalling and breathtaking; but spread over three centuries and related to the total population of West Africa such figures become more nearly comparable to those for more or less voluntary emigration from certain parts of Europe, such as the Scottish Highlands. And the impact seems to have been heaviest in those areas, such as Dahomey, the Niger delta, the Congo, which were already most densely populated. There seems little evidence to show that the population loss led, in most areas under consideration

[15] J. Suret-Canale, *Afrique Noire* (Paris, 1958), I, p. 69.
[16] C. Wrigley, "Speculations on the Economic Prehistory of Africa," *JAH* I (1960), 203.

here, to a demographic crisis, or to such widespread shortages of labor as would *directly* inhibit economic growth.

It is more difficult to generalize about its indirect effects in disrupting social relationships within African society, or in causing wars. As suggested above, such effects seem to have been more serious in Dahomey than in Senegal or Guinea. "Traditional African society" varied considerably in the first place, and the impact of the slave trade was not uniform either. In some states the chief effect may have been to provide channels for disposing profitably of such socially undesirable people as prisoners of war, suspected witches, convicts, or insolvent debtors. Rarely if ever did it lead to the breakdown of authority and the return of a Hobbesian "state of nature." Everywhere, among both forest and savanna peoples, among both animists and Muslims, there was a respected body of law or custom which controlled the rights and status of slaves; everywhere those slaves who might properly be sold were distinguished from household or domestic slaves, entitled to own property, to marry free persons and beget free offspring, to achieve their own freedom by various methods, in some societies to rise to positions of wealth and great authority. Even in regions like Dahomey, where the growth of European demand stimulated efforts to provide supplies by military campaigns or marauding raids against neighboring peoples, the rights of "domestic" slaves continued to be respected within their own society. Certainly confidence and free movement between neighboring peoples were often impeded; but that neither disappeared altogether is shown by the way the *dyulas* continued to move with more beneficial merchandise throughout most of the forest belt. To some extent indeed their activities may actually have been stimulated by the prospect of selling not only salt, gold, and kola, but some of their surplus porters. The slave trade did not produce uncontrolled disorder, but imposed its own system of commercial conventions and practices on African society.

In the excitement of understanding this, historians may forget to inquire more deeply into the effect of that system. Even if "panyarring"—the acquiring of slaves by abduction or violence—was in most places not practiced by responsible slave-dealers, there were plenty of Europeans and Africans willing to indulge in it where the local ruler was not strong enough to forbid them. In some places this may have added a very real hazard to African life; the Fula cattle-trader from Futa Toro who was seized and sold off to Maryland in 1730 was exceptional only in that his case became documented and well known. But even in the case of slaves who were sold as prisoners-of-war, witches, thieves, or adulterers, it does not necessarily close the matter to point out that their equivalents in contemporary Europe might equally well be transported, if not put to death. Eighteenth-century enemies of the trade argued that growing demands for slaves might lead to men being deemed eligible for sale who would otherwise have remained free. That African "wars" were sometimes deliberately contrived slave raids—that men were sometimes enticed into adultery, or deliberately denounced as witches, may be readily accepted; to suppose otherwise would be to attribute to Africa a capacity for remaining uncorrupted by the temptations of a market economy which no other continent has shown. How many military campaigns were started for this purpose, how often convicts were "framed," remain as questions to which evidence may never permit precise answers.

But appraisal of the effects of the Atlantic slave trade does not depend solely on such points. Economically, its apologists rest on the classical liberal argument that commercial exchanges benefit both parties to them; but in important particulars the slave trade may be an exception. So far as the argument assumes that both parties receive goods which they desire and could not economically have produced for themselves, it may perhaps be admitted; but it can hardly be held that the goods provided by the Europeans were such as to enhance very greatly the quality of African life. The items in demand varied considerably along the coast (most African consumers knew what they wanted and were reluctant to accept substitutes); but in the seventeenth and eighteenth centuries the bulk of West Africa's imports were cheap European or Indian manufactures intended for consumption or display: hardware, beads, and cheap jewellery, above all clothing and textiles. Dahomeans usually demanded part payment in cowrie shells imported from the Indian Ocean, which were acceptable as currency over a wide area. Tobacco might also be in demand. The market for spirits varied—always virtually nil in Muslim Mauritania, it was developed elsewhere through the familiar custom of providing refreshment for the brokers during the actual bargaining process; but contrary to legend, alcohol played a smaller part in the slave trade than in the later period of "legitimate commerce." Firearms and gunpowder were more important for their political and social effects than for their cash value. Such articles had not been common in the Saharan trade and the flintlocks now introduced were rarely very destructive, except sometimes to the marksman himself; but, selectively supplied, they much increased the military capacity of the littoral peoples, and might, as in Dahomey, change the balance of power among African states. Parodying Marx, it might be suggested that changes in the method of destruction have often provided the motor of historical development. In fact the only African industry actually fostered by the slave trade seems to have been the manufacture of gunpowder, apparently well established in Senegambia by the eighteenth century. For the most striking feature to emerge from study of the outward cargo manifests of slave ships is the absence of any productive tool more important than a machete. The effect of commerce was to encourage conspicuous consumption by the few rather than investment in the development of resources.

For this there was another reason peculiar to the slave trade. In other commerce, it may reasonably be assumed that some at least of those who profit will be moved by capitalistic urges to reinvest their accumulated wealth in projects intended to increase productive capacity. But the trade in human labor, resting on the export of one of the essential factors of production, was inherently likely to pervert this tendency. This is neatly illustrated by a Sarakulé engaged in the internal slave trade who in 1878 told the French traveller Soleillet that he indeed aimed to accumulate capital—with the aim not of starting new productive enterprises, but of buying three or four men and a woman for his own service, and settling down to let their labor maintain him in relative idleness.[17] Economically, the greatest condemnation of the slave trade is not so much that the terms of trade were unfavorable to the Africans (they tended to improve with the passage of time); but that export of human labor was in itself liable to distort, if not to prevent, diversification of production and economic growth. With all respect to Mr. Wrigley's argument, its expansion cannot really be considered to have enriched the lives of the forest peoples. Such trade may possibly have broadened their horizons, but their backs still remained firmly turned toward the rising sun of the scientific and technological age.

[17] J. Paul Soleillet, *Voyage à Ségou* (Paris, 1887), p. 177.

FOUR

THE MUSLIM RESURGENCE

After the Moroccan invasion of Songhai in 1591, Islamic influence in West Africa suffered erosion and dilution. Some territories formerly under Muslims reverted to the rule of animists, like the Bambara dynasties of Ségou and Kaarta; in others, such as the Hausa states, the enforcement of Koranic law and practice became lax. Even more than formerly, the maintenance of Islam depended on the congregations of the mosques of the trading towns, and on the missionary influence of the *dyulas*; and our scanty evidence does not suggest that either group was in a flourishing religious condition during the seventeenth and eighteenth centuries. In Timbuktu the native *ulama* were persecuted by the Moroccan invaders as potentially subversive elements; moreover much of the desert trade had been diverted to more easterly routes, terminating in Bornu and Hausaland, so the western commercial towns tended to decline in importance. As for the *dyulas*, their links with orthodox Islam were often remote and their teaching unsophisticated and scrappy. In this period, one modern writer believes, "Islam was neutralized by being emptied of all challenge to African ways of life and Muslims were accommodated into Negro society." [1]

It is always difficult to assess fairly such charges of spiritual degeneracy. In Senegambia, the only Muslim area under continuous European observation, canonical prayers, fasts, and festivals still seem to have been fairly regularly observed, although one observer noted that "the substantial" were more devout than "the vulgar sort." [2] This area too was distinguished by a commercial demand for paper, but this seems to have been used less for literary work than

---

[1] J. Spencer Trimingham, *History of Islam in West Africa* (Glasgow, 1962), p. 141.
[2] J. J. Lemaire, *Les Voyages du Sieur le Maire* (Paris, 1695), p. 91.

for making amulets or *grigris*—fragmentary Koranic texts sold for their magical value to animists as well as Muslims. The Moors to the north of the Senegal river remained notably more devout than the Negro peoples to the south; among the Wolof in particular political divisions and commercial influences were accompanied by lapses from orthodox practice which were not reversed until the nineteenth century.

But it would be an error to assume that even "nominal religion" is insignificant. Through much of the savanna Islam retained, as the attenuated legacy of the medieval empires, a core of earnest adherents, and a more widely diffused capital of prestige and influence which in the eighteenth century provided bases for striking advances by militant reformers, comparable to those made in other parts of the Muslim world. In almost all of these the prime movers were Fulas (French name *Peuls*) or related peoples speaking their language.

The origins of this distinctive-looking people have been the subject of some highly speculative controversy; but archaeological and linguistic evidence strongly suggests that after the desiccation of the Sahara they settled in the extreme Western Sudan, probably in the Senegal valley.[3] By the eighteenth century Fulas had become dispersed through the savanna region, as far west as Wadai, sometimes forming states, but generally living as herdsmen who pastured their cattle by consent of those who held the land. Not all were Muslims, but many of those who had settled in towns were notable for their piety and scholarship. These Fulas made their most famous mark on African history in the *jihad*, or holy war, launched in 1804 by 'Uthman dan Fodio in the Hausa state of Gobir. But in recent years western scholars have learned to place this within a longer series of Islamic advances, which created the first genuine theocratic states in West Africa. Social discontent, ethnic feeling among underprivileged Fulas, discontent with existing governments, seem to have been among the preconditions which favored all these movements; for success each depended on one or more dynamic leaders, devout and learned in the Muslim faith, brave and skillful on the battlefield, and dedicated to re-creating the ideal Muslim society of the founders of Islam.

[3] On the contentious problem of Fula origins, see the Introduction to Derrick J. Stenning, *Savannah Nomads* (London, 1959).

In Futa Jalon, an upland district in the modern Republic of Guinea, Muslim Fulas began to settle as herdsmen during the seventeenth century. The ruling *Jalonke* (a branch of the Susu people) apparently gave some nominal adherence to Islam, but by 1725 they were at odds with orthodox Fulas over the survival of certain animist practices, and the relationship between the *Imam* (as leader of the Muslim community) and the chiefs. A *jihad* was launched by *karamoko* [Reverend] Alfa Ibrahima, but fifty years of struggle were needed before the Muslims, under the military leadership of Ibrahima Sori, secured control of Futa Jalon and the immediately neighboring districts. Their victory meant the imposition of theocratic authority on the decentralized structure of provincial government which previously existed; later a curious constitution was devised under which descendants of the two great *jihad* leaders alternated in power as *Imam*, or *Alimami*, for two years at a time. This state was not very formidable militarily, but its influence over its neighbors was strong and far-reaching. Many of the refugees from Futa Jalon, and some of the peoples among whom they settled near the Guinea coast, acknowledged the nominal overlordship of the *Alimamies*, and paid them tribute; other migrants to the interior took with them more or less adulterated forms of Muslim belief and custom.

The advance of Muslim rule involved the extension, not only of legal and ethical systems based on the Shari'a, but of authentic though diluted traces of Islamic cosmopolitanism. The assurance of protection and justice according to familiar principles seems to have encouraged the movement of caravan traders toward the Guinea coast: Futa Jalon became a meeting place for the commercial systems of savanna and forest. Europeans noted that Muslim towns were larger than those of Temnes and Buloms, protected by walls or bamboo palisades; even their traditional circular houses were "more lofty and spacious," and built of sun-baked brick. It is only a feeble echo of the architectural tradition associated with es-Saheli and Timbuktu, but it may be an authentic one. But the most striking distinguishing marks of the converted countries were the assiduous attendance of children at Koranic schools, the high value attached by their elders to books and manuscripts, and the regularity of all in prayer. The first European visitors to Futa Jalon noted in 1794 that its inhabitants "attend to the ceremonial duties of their religion with such strictness

as might well cause Christians to blush," [4] and a modern authority
regards the influence of this state as "the primary factor leading to
a diffusion of Islam throughout western Guinea." [5]

The Muslims of Futa Jalon also had contacts with those of Futa
Toro, a confederation of small states which occupied roughly the
same part of the lower Senegal valley as the ancient Muslim state
of Tekrur. Its population, largely composed of Fula-speaking people
called Tokolors (a name derived from Tekrur), was the subject during the eighteenth century of a struggle between the forces of Islamic
orthodoxy and the laxer policies practiced by its Fula overlord the
siratik. (These rulers did not lapse completely into animism, and in
1682 the *siratik* was noted as "observing the precepts of Mahomet
more religiously than the other Negroes." [6]) The forces of orthodoxy
were represented partly by *marabouts* from Mauritania, partly by
aristocratic Tokolor clerics known as *torodbe*. In 1776, as the *jihad*
finally triumphed in Futa Jalon, a *torodo* called Suleiman Bal who
had studied there launched an attack on animist practices in Futa
Toro. This struggle was over quickly; the *torodbe* secured power
throughout the states and elected an *alimami* for the whole confederation from among their number. But his power remained relatively
small compared to that of the state-chiefs. European observers, perhaps drawing analogies with another revolution of 1776, commonly
described the constitution as "republican." [7]

From Futa Toro also the prestige of the victorious Muslims spread
far afield. Rulers of Bondou and Khasso, on the route to Futa Jalon,
declared their conversion; the armies of Futa Toro called on Wolofs
to rise against unrighteous rulers, finding liberty in submission to the
law of Muhammed; individual Fulas in the service of French traders
assisted the advance of their religion as far afield as Port Loko in
Sierra Leone.[8] Its most important effect may have been to stimulate
the zeal of expatriate *torodbe* settled in Hausa country: one of these

[4] Thomas Winterbottom, *An Account of the Native Africans in the Neighbour-
hood of Sierra Leone* (London, 1803), I, 85-8, 168-72, 209-10, 217-21, 230-5.

[5] J. Spencer Trimingham, *Islam in West Africa* (London, 1959), p. 18. There
is an impressive collection of literature from Futa Jalon in the *Fonds Gilbert
Vieillard* at I.F.A.N., Dakar, where it is being studied by M. Tierno Diallo.

[6] Lemaire, *op. cit.*, p. 54.

[7] Dominique Harcourt Lamiral, *L'Afrique et le peuple affriquain* (Paris, 1789),
pp. 174-5.

[8] Amadu Wurie, "The Bundukas of Sierra Leone," *Sierra Leone Studies* n.s. 1.
(Freetown, 1953).

men, 'Uthman dan Fodio, launched the most important and successful of the *jihads* in 1804. But although the empire which he founded
at Sokoto influenced territories now within the Republic of Niger, its
most far-reaching consequences form part of the history of Nigeria
rather than of the countries under discussion here.[9]

Another chain reaction followed. Among the followers of 'Uthman
dan Fodio there may have been numbered for a time Sekou Amadu
Hammadi Boubou of Macina, a Fula state on the middle Niger whose
rulers paid tribute to the animist Bambaras of Ségou. The exact relationship between these two men requires further study; but when,
about 1818, Sekou Amadu began his drive to restore Macina to the
true faith, he clearly looked to Sokoto for inspiration, and at times
for advice. He was also influenced by the spiritual teachings of the
Qadiriyya, a Sufite *tarikh*, or fraternity. Within a few years Sekou
Amadu controlled yet another theocratic state, extending along the
middle Niger from Ségou to the western marches of Sokoto.

Like other *jihad* leaders, Amadu founded a new walled capital at
the scene of his *hegira*, naming it Hamdallahi (or "Praise God").
Its great mosque contrasted by the austerity of its design with that
of the old commercial city of Jenné, which eventually Amadu caused
to be destroyed. Here there met the grand council which Amadu
constituted and to whom he would defer on questions of public policy
and the interpretation of Muslim law. For though he remained the
venerated leader of the state, his government was openly based on
orthodox Malikite interpretations of the *Shari'a*: recently recorded
traditions emphasize that this was the touchstone of the council's
debates on many issues of public policy. Although animist customs
not prohibited by the Koran might be tolerated the general spirit of
government was austere and puritanical; converts were required not
only to conform in public worship, and in such matters as the veiling
of women, but to abstain from fermented liquor and tobacco (which
"poisons the breath, darkens the teeth, and doesn't fill the stomach").
Public celebrations were restricted to religious festivals and state oc-
casions. The policing of Hamdallahi was entrusted to a commission
of seven *marabouts*, whose professed standards of public hygiene

[9] See the volume in this series by Dr. John E. Flint, *Nigeria and Ghana*, pp.
99-105. For evidence of Sokoto's influence in Niger, see *West Africa*, Nov. 28,
1964, p. 1335, profile of Amadou Seydou, Ambassador to Paris and London
of the Republic of Niger. His grandfather [sic] is said to have been Imam and
counsellor to 'Uthman dan Fodio.

could be compared most favorably with those of any contemporary European city. Girls as well as boys were supposed to attend school at the age of seven, if one was available. The syllabus seems to have been conservative, with study of the Koran, the commentaries, the Hadith, predominating: the "auxiliary sciences" of Islamic scholarship were not usually taught. Altogether the rulers of Macina seem to have been less learned and scholarly than those of Sokoto or Futa Jalon; but their austere regime seem to have commanded lasting devotion, in particular from their Fula subjects.[10]

This devotion was not felt by all their subjects; in many places the empire of Macina depended on military force. In the north, around the ancient religious and commercial town of Timbuktu, it had continually to face disaffection from the Tuareg, the *arma* (descendants of the Moroccan conquerors of 1591) and especially from the Kunta Arabs of Timbuktu, who regarded the new state as an upstart power ruled by an inferior people of questionable religious authority. The Fulas conquered Timbuktu in 1826 after the state council had resolved that the people of the province were bound to pay *zekkat* to Macina, but the authority of the Kunta remained considerable; throughout its life the empire had to reckon with their proud and principled insubordination on many questions affecting the proper exercise of their authority. In the west too there was continuing hostility from the Bambara states of Ségou and Kaarta—hostility in which a strong sense of ethnic identity was reinforced by reluctance to modify traditional customs and meet the rigorous demands of orthodox Islam.

Sekou Amadu and his successors succeeded in reunifying a substantial section of the former dependencies of Songhai. Yet, partly because of the decline in importance of trade through the western Sahara, its resources were never so great. Although, about 1830, a grateful merchant of Jenné could rejoice that his caravans were again reaching Kong in all security, the economy of the upper and even the middle Niger valley was beginning to reorient itself toward the Atlantic coast and Macina was becoming a backwater. Already double-barrelled flintlocks supplied by Senegalese merchants were common

[10] This account is based upon the oral traditions of Macina, recorded and published in Amadou Hampaté Ba and Jacques Daget, *L'Empire peul du Macina*, Vol. I (Dakar, 1955), especially pp. 45-68.

at Timbuktu; it is not clear how effectively they were used in the Macina *jihad*, but in future wars their role would be very important.

Macina was certainly a more strongly centralized theocracy than either of the Futas; its attempts to enforce its puritanical standards made a lasting impression on some at least of its subjects. But among others it aroused resistance, and sharpened ethnic antagonisms. Opposition came not only from animists holding to their ancestral beliefs, but from alternative interpreters of Muslim orthodoxy. From the mid-nineteenth century Macina had to face the rise of a rival Muslim empire whose leader, Al Hajj 'Umar al Tall, not only presented an alternative charismatic appeal, but had in some ways a more modern political outlook. Aware of the growing importance of the new coastal supply routes. 'Umar so planned his operations as to take advantage of them.

'Umar was a Tokolor, born in Futa Toro toward the end of the eighteenth century. His father was a *marabout*, and 'Umar was educated in the Tijaniyya, a new Sufite fraternity which reached his homeland from the Maghreb through the Trarzas of Mauritania in the later eighteenth century. To an uninstructed outsider, this seems not unlike a Muslim equivalent of Calvinism. By virtue of verbal communications from Muhammed to the founder, members of the Tijaniyya claimed to have been chosen for a special dispensation of Divine grace setting them apart from other Muslims; yet in West Africa they fought to make this spiritual privilege available to all. Teaching the faithful a few simple texts and formulae as the essentials of belief, the Tijaniyya held more egalitarian principles than the clerical aristocracy who had triumphed in 1776.

After studying with Koranic scholars from Mauritania and Futa Jalon, 'Umar set out on the *haj* about 1826. In Arabia his unusual learning won him the confidence of the leader of the Tijaniyya, and 'Umar was invested as *Khalifa* of the order for the Western Sudan. After three visits to Mecca and a period at Al-azhar in Cairo 'Umar returned to visit the great Muslim capitals of West Africa. He married wives from the families of both El Kanami of Bornu and Muhammad Bello of Sokoto. About 1838 he returned to Hamdallahi; Sekou Amadu had previously not been unfriendly toward the Tijaniyya, but now some hostility entered their relations. Macina traditions ascribe this to the Kunta, fearful for their own standing as leaders of the Qadiriyya and aware of conflicts which had taken place between the two orders in the Maghreb.[11] So after another uneasy visit to the Bambaras of Ségou, 'Umar settled in Futa Jalon where the prestige gained by his travels and studies attracted many followers.

In 1846-7 'Umar visited his homeland on the lower Senegal, where his preaching—summarized by hostile observers in the words, "You are like the unfaithful, eating and drinking injustice, and your chiefs violate God's law by oppressing the weak"—attracted new disciples, or *talibés*. Soon afterwards he performed a *hegira* to Dinguiray, just to the east of Futa Jalon, where he began to build up economic and military resources. Devout Muslims, and less devout individuals on the make, came to join him, some bringing offerings which were used to buy firearms on the coast. (Not the least proof of 'Umar's state-craft was this appreciation that in view of the relative decline of the desert commerce on which earlier empires had rested it was necessary to look to the Atlantic for trade and armaments.) By converting persons in authority, by inciting their subjects against them, or by direct conquest, 'Umar gradually extended his territorial base. During the early 1850s he took control of many small Bambara or Mandinka principalities in the upper Niger and Senegal valleys; he then made war on the larger Bambara states on Kaarta and Ségou, and established his capital in the latter city in 1861.

On the whole these early successes were gained against animists, whose earlier Islamization had left only syncretic traces. Among these peoples orthodox and sometimes unpopular Koranic teaching was enforced: women were segregated, men were rationed to four wives, heads were shaved, and fermented liquors prohibited. When 'Umar turned against those who were Muslims already, he was less uniformly successful. Although he attracted many *talibés* from his homeland of Futa Toro, the ruling *torodbe* remained hostile to his subversive heresies; he never controlled their country, and his moves in this direction caused collisions with the French. After the conquest of Ségou 'Umar turned instead against Macina and destroyed Hamdallahi in 1862: but he did not succeed in repressing either the ethnic consciousness of the Fulas or the sectarian consciousness of the Qadiriyya.

Although 'Umar's claim to be the spiritual and military leader of

---

[11] *Ibid.*, pp. 233-48. On the Tijaniyya in general and the career of Al Hajj 'Umar in particular, see Jamil M. Abun-Nasr, *The Tijaniyya* (London, 1965).

West African Islam was thus not undisputed, his influence extended far beyond the boundaries of his empire. Three of his disciples played particularly important roles in the history of Senegambia in the later nineteenth century. Maba, born in Badibu of a family from Futa Toro, in 1862-67 launched a *jihad* which led to the extension of Islamic influence in many of the lands bordering the Gambia valley.[12] He in turn converted Lat-Dior, *damel* of Cayor 1862-82, who, working with peasants and *marabouts* against the animist freebooters known as *tiédos*, was largely responsible for reconverting his Wolof subjects to full acceptance of Islam.[13] The Sarakulé Mamadu Lamina, who resisted France in the upper Senegal valley in the later 1880s, was also a disciple of 'Umar.

In the lands which he controlled directly 'Umar displayed notable qualities of statecraft. Particularly notable was his success in utilizing the skills of African Muslims who had worked in European settlements as smiths, masons, carpenters, or traders to strengthen the army and the administration which was improvised in the conquered provinces. Yet given the state of communications and technology, central control over such a large area was necessarily difficult to maintain. By 1863 the unity of the new state was threatened by revolts both of the Qadiri Fulas of Macina (aided by the Kunta Arabs) and by Bambaras and other conquered peoples reasserting their ethnic identity and their animist beliefs. After his death in 1864 his son and successor Amadu had to deal with further revolts by both Muslims and animists, and also by provincial governors and kinsmen reluctant to acknowledge an undivided succession. To some observers, the Tokolor ruling class founded by 'Umar seemed destined to be quickly overthrown by internal divisions and the revolt of subject peoples. Nevertheless, Amadu (who, though he lacked his father's religious charisma, showed considerable political acumen and skill) retained much of his authority for another thirty years, until the empire was finally destroyed by the superior military technology of France.

A final phase in the history of independent Muslim states in the Western Sudan will be discussed later: that of the *empires combattantes* (as M. Gouilly has called them), the most important of

[12] Tamsir Dusmane Ba, "Essai historique sur le Rip," *Bulletin de l'IFAN*, series B, xix, 1957.

[13] Vincent Monteil, "Lat-Dior, *Damel* du Kayor et l'Islamisation des Wolofs," *Archives de Sociologie des Religions*, XVI, 1963, pp. 77-104. See below Ch. 6, p. 94.

which was founded by the Mandinka warrior Samori. These leaders have been dismissed by some writers as ambitious military adventurers, honored by others as leaders of anticolonial resistance; their political astuteness was more evident than the intellectual and spiritual qualities of earlier Muslim state-builders, but in some respects they were carrying on their work. They too claimed to be *Imams*, seeking to order society according to truer Islamic models; they too struggled, in this process, to establish wider territorial units; in practice they too might appeal to ethnic loyalties which were potentially divisive. Mutual antagonisms among the Muslim states prevented them from cooperating effectively in the face of European advances.

All the same, it is easy to exaggerate the disunity and disorder of the Western Sudan at the time of the French occupation. The economic, technological, and administrative resources of Muslim empires might be unequal to the demands of the imperialist period, but their institutions often rested on solid bases on which the French, had they chosen, might have built at least as effectively as the British did in Sokoto. Their work of religious proselytization was much more durable; although many converts of Al Hajj 'Umar rejected Islam as soon as they were able, many others remained as loyally attached to the Tijaniyya as did many subjects of Macina to the Qadiriyya. But these sectarian divisions will probably prove a less important legacy of the nineteenth century than the fervent acceptance by substantial populations of a world religion which they are conscious of sharing with many millions of Africans and Asians.

FIVE

THE FRENCH PRESENCE

It was probably during the 1520s that French merchants from Dieppe began to make regular voyages to the West African coast, seeking to exploit the commercial prospects which Portuguese enterprise had revealed to Europeans. Until 1580 Kings of France were inhibited in their desire to support their sailors by the diplomatic expediency of avoiding an open challenge to Portugal's claim of monopoly, but "interlopers" continued to sail from several French ports, both on peaceful trading journeys and to make privateering attacks on Portuguese ships. Until the wars of religion temporarily checked their activities in the later sixteenth century, Huguenots from La Rochelle were active in the African trade. Already French traders tended to concentrate on the area of Cape Verde; by 1566 some of its Wolof chiefs spoke French and looked to Frenchmen for advice on their relations with other Europeans. But French ships also went as far afield as Angola and the Congo.

After 1624 Norman merchants began to form joint-stock companies to develop their African interests on a more long-term basis. Shortly afterward Cardinal Richelieu began the policy of granting extensive privileges and monopolies for trade within specified territories, trusting that the money and initiative of these Companies would increase the power and wealth of the French state. Such concessions were of course not necessarily recognized or respected by foreigners, but, legally at least, they precluded the wasteful expense of competition with other French traders. Some Frenchmen began to erect permanent buildings near the mouth of the Senegal river. The first attempt was made in 1638; in 1659 the French moved to a firmer site on the island of Guet N'Dar, well within the sandbar of the estuary, where they founded the fort and settlement of Saint-Louis.

In 1664 the mercantilist alliance between private capital and the French state was taken a stage further. Colbert, the famous finance minister of Louis XIV, revoked a number of concessions for trade in the Atlantic previously held by companies of merchants from the outports and concentrated them in a new West India Company; since this was supported by Parisian financiers, it was hoped it might more easily mobilize the nation's capital for the great trade war against Dutch and English. A high priority was the development of sugar plantations in the French West Indies, so that French foreign exchange need no longer be used to buy Brazilian sugar in Iberian markets. If such plantations were to flourish independently of Dutch finance and shipping, the Company would have to provide them with an independent supply of African labor, and this was to be the primary aim of its African operations.

French resources of finance and shipping were far inferior to those of the Dutch and these schemes proved overambitious; the West India Company was soon in difficulties and was liquidated in 1672. While the Antilles passed under more direct royal control, a new Senegal Company was founded to take over its privileges in Senegal, Cape Verde, and the Gambia. The Dutch war of 1672-78 provided the French government with an opportunity to expel the Dutch, not indeed as the slaving interest hoped from their position on the Gold Coast, but from Arguin (which they had occupied in 1638) and from the fortified island of Gorée, near Cape Verde, which they had occupied since 1588. This was an important entrepôt, a base for trade on the so-called *petit-côte* (where Europeans had long traded with Cayor at Rufisque, with Baol at Portudal, and with Sine at Joal) and also a convenient point for ships going southward to stock up with food for the slaves they hoped to acquire. Although Dutch interlopers, sometimes operating under the Brandenburg flag, maintained a strong position in the Mauritanian gum trade until 1727, France now held a relatively firm territorial base in the Senegal region; and it was here that a long series of privileged Companies concentrated their efforts.

Colbert and his successors intended that the Companies operating in Africa should in the first place provide a regular supply of slaves for the development of the new sugar plantations in the French West Indies (and also for Royal galleys in the Mediterranean). M. Abdoulaye Ly emphasizes that the Senegal Company, several times reconstituted before the end of the seventeenth century, concentrated on fulfilling this demand; though he supplies evidence of its interest in a variety of other commodities and projects, he holds that it remained *avant tout négrière*.[1] Nevertheless, its success in obtaining slaves fell far short of expectations; the Company lacked the capital necessary if it was to multiply its voyages or push them far beyond Senegal. But here the supply of slaves remained limited, for reasons already discussed; and in any case Senegalese were regarded as less satisfactory plantation workers than Africans from the Gold and Slave Coasts.[2] The use which successive Companies made of their monopoly thus came under increasing criticism—from agents of the State, from the rising sugar interests, and also from the merchants of developing outports, such as Nantes, who hoped to profit from greater freedom in the slave trade. The French state began to experiment with different expedients for entering the great slave markets further south, while her posts in the Senegal gradually acquired economic and social characteristics of their own.

France's attempts to establish herself in the slave markets of the Bight of Benin are more interesting to students of European economic growth than to historians of Africa. Although ultimately France achieved second or third place among the slaving nations, supplying her insatiable plantations in the Antilles with perhaps twenty thousand Africans a year, this was largely the work of private traders or of local consortia who had neither the means nor the need to maintain permanent establishments in Africa. The privileged companies of the seventeenth century did indeed make several attempts to establish bases on the Slave, Gold, and Ivory Coasts, and sometimes, as at Assinie in 1701, these were accompanied by Catholic missionaries; but with one exception they were abandoned after a few years, leaving few discernible effects on the history of the country. The exception was at Whydah, where the West India Company, after failing to secure exclusive privileges in Allada, established a factory about 1671. At first this post was apparently not very active. In 1694 Thomas Phillips found two Frenchmen living "dejected and poor" in a little mudhouse; having seen no French ship for three or four years, they had

---

[1] Abdoulaye Ly, *La Compagnie du Sénégal* (Paris, 1958), pp. 198, 293-4.
[2] See above, p. 37.

been driven back on Whydah's public assistance.[3] In 1704 a more respectable "fort" was erected, which under the successive direction of the *Compagnie des Indes* and the French Crown provided a foothold for intervention in Aja politics and for participation in Dahomean slave markets. But during the eighteenth century only temporary shifts in local policy distinguished the French role from that of her European rivals, and few foundations were laid for any lasting French influence in the life of Dahomey. Two hundred or so Dahomeans worked in the French fort, but they seem to have been little affected by the ministrations of the dispirited chaplains who were occasionally appointed to serve the few Frenchmen and mulattoes, or by any other experience of French culture. The Company, tired of being taken in by *soi-disant* "African princes," discouraged the practice of bringing a few Africans to Paris for education, and in 1788 few of France's Dahomean employees spoke French.[4] Only in Senegal did eighteenth-century French commercial enterprise have much enduring influence.

France in Senegal

The Senegal river attracted mercantilists as a route to the interior which could easily be monopolized by the power controlling its mouth. But it has many disadvantages as a commercial waterway. Shifting sandbars at the estuary make entry difficult for all vessels and impossible for those drawing more than nine feet of water. There is great seasonal variation in the level of the river; generally it is only in July and August that trading craft can travel the full six hundred miles up to the Félou falls (near the modern town of Kayes). But in West Africa, even these opportunities for navigation were exceptional; until Europeans finally discovered the Niger's course in 1830, only the Gambia offered better prospects of access to the interior. In fact, throughout the seventeenth and eighteenth centuries, some European clung to the theory that the Senegal and Gambia were twin mouths of the Niger (which Leo Africanus had erroneously described as flowing to the west).

The more enterprising Frenchmen who served at Saint-Louis were thus led to hope that by the river they might obtain access, if not to

[3] Thomas Phillips, A *Journal of a Voyage Made in the Hannibal of London,* Ann. 1693, 1694, in A. & J. Churchill, *Voyages,* Vol. VI (1744); cf. Ly, *op. cit.,* p. 265n.
[4] I. A. Akinjogbin, *Dahomey,* p. 168: P. Labarthe, *Voyage à la Côte de Guinée,* Paris, An XI (1803), pp. 111, 165.

the Niger itself, at least to the slave markets which supplied the British in the Gambia, and to the gold mines of Bambouk, which sent tantalizing small consignments to the coast. The first attempt to travel upriver seems to date from the 1680s and although the people of Futa Toro tried to stop Europeans from passing through to their neighbors, some of them reached Félou. In 1693 Chambonneau, a former director of the Company's concession, sketched out an ambitious plan envisaging not only the occupation of territory by the French state and the development of cultivation by French immigrants, but contacts with the interior, Timbuktu and beyond.[5] The Frenchman generally regarded as having first developed a coherent Senegalese policy is André Brüe, who was in charge of the concession in 1697-1702 and 1714-20, and returned several times thereafter on missions of inspection. His eulogist Labat attributed to Brüe journeys and writings made by his predecessor la Courbe, and it is possible that some French historians have exaggerated his originality; but he does seem to have developed a more coherent African policy than his predecessors. His dealings with peoples of the lower valley appear to have been more tactfully conducted, and his attention to the back country more sustained. It was Brüe who established the first French "forts" in Galam and sponsored reconnaissances of gold deposits in lower Bambouk. But the gold proved less abundant than Europeans hoped; and to the physical and environmental difficulties of inland penetration was added the opposition of Africans involved in existing patterns of commerce. So these outposts, sporadically maintained, abandoned, re-sited during the two centuries before effective French occupation, fulfilled only very partially the underlying hopes of attracting to the Senegal a growing trade in gold, slaves, and other commodities unspecified.

From the point of view of trading profits, France's alternative line of development proved more successful; this was to extend the coast trade based on Gorée southwards into the Gambia, the Casamance, and the centers of Portuguese activity at Bissao and Cacheo. About 1678 the French established a small trading post at Albreda in the Gambia, where they intermittently maintained a foothold until 1857; its purpose was to compete with the fort of the English Royal Africa Company on James Island in purchasing slaves and gold brought down by *dyulas* from Bambouk and beyond. It does not seem to have

[5] Ly, *op. cit.*, pp. 257-63.

been very successful in this; nor did either Company gain much by resorting to armed conflict. During the wars of 1689-1713 French and English forts in Senegambia were in turn captured and recaptured. To avoid wasteful hostility the Companies at times attempted to neutralize Senegambia, remaining at peace with each other and where necessary cooperating against their African neighbors; henceforth Anglo-French rivalry in Senegambia tended to alternate with periods of quite close local cooperation. By an agreement of May 25, 1740, for example, the Director of the Senegal concession and the Governor of the Gambia not only agreed to respect each other's African interests (as they continued to do through the first years of the war of Austrian Succession), but to exchange supplies of those commodities which each was best placed to obtain—300 slaves from the Gambia against 360,000 pounds of Senegalese gum.[6] That Senegambia formed a natural region which could only be satisfactorily developed as a whole, where Anglo-French rivalry could damage the interests of both Africans and Europeans, has thus been recognized for over 250 years; but statesmen have rarely managed to act consistently on this assumption, or for long. During the Seven Years War, the War of the American Revolution, the Revolutionary and Napoleonic wars Senegambia was still, sporadically, a theater of operations.

As far as Saint-Louis was concerned, much of its value lay in its access to supplies of gum, a product still essential for various printing and finishing processes of the growing textile industries of Europe, as well as for pharmaceutical use. The Mauritanian forests north of the Senegal provided a large part of the world supply; if France could monopolize its export, she would be able to sell to competitors at her own prices, and would be much strengthened in the mercantilist struggle for trade. Unfortunately for her the Trarza Moors (though not the Braknas, whose lands lay inland) had two possible markets available; they could take their gum to the trading posts known as *escales* on the Senegal river, maritime access to which could be controlled from Saint-Louis, or they could take it to Arguin or Portendic on the barren and waterless coast of Mauritania, where French supervision was much more difficult. Unfortunately it was at the coast that the Trarzas preferred to sell most of their gum until well into the nine-

---

[6] Delcourt, *Etablissements*, pp. 341-3; cf. J. M. Gray, *History of the Gambia* (Cambridge, 1940), pp. 208-13.

teenth century; partly because the Dutch who traded there treated them more generously and tactfully than the French, partly from a simple economic appreciation of the advantage of promoting competition among buyers. In 1727 the Dutch Government eventually agreed to recognize the right of exclusive trade which France claimed along the whole coast from Cape Blanco to Sierra Leone; but by now English ships were appearing to trade at Arguin and Portendic, sometimes under naval protection, and the struggle for the Gum Coast became a recurrent minor theme of Anglo-French maritime and colonial rivalry. From the point of view of African history, the significant point is the failure of all French attempts to dominate the situation by pressure on the Trarzas. Whether they sought their cooperation by agreement (as when Brüe made an agreement with Emir Ali Chandora in 1717) or by force (as in 1738, when French guns tried to stop the trade at Portendic by firing, not on the English but on the unsuspecting Moors who were trading with them) the French were never able to impose their will for long. Their relations with the Mauritanians remained essentially those of buyer and seller; and the Trarzas assumed that the French need for their gum was greater than their need of French trade goods. Until the midnineteenth century, when European demand fell off and this coastal trade came to a natural end, they seem to have been right.

Still, French companies did profit from the gum trade: also in much lesser degrees from dealing in gold, ivory, and hides, as well as from their disappointingly modest business in slaves. This relative diversity, as well as the possibility of limited penetration inland, gave their Senegalese establishments a distinctive character. Like the forts of the Gold and Slave Coasts they were extraterritorial enclaves in Africa, governed on European principles yet numbering Africans among their permanent inhabitants, and influenced in their internal development by their relations with African neighbors, landlords, and customers. But in Senegal, unlike the Gold Coast, Europeans did not wait for trade to come to them, but went up the river and down the coast to look for it. They were thus more widely, though not necessarily more harmoniously, involved in the life of their region. During the eighteenth century the Senegalese towns of Saint-Louis and Gorée saw the growth of small but influential communities which were Afro-European in culture, and to some extent genetically also.

The African population of these settlements was recruited in four main ways. In the first place successive French administrations found it expedient to employ Africans. There were usually somewhere between 100 and 250 Frenchmen in the Senegalese "concession," serving as traders, accountants, and officials; surgeons and chaplains; artisans, laborers, seamen, and soldiers. But conditions of service were rarely attractive to men of talent or good character; Senegal was regarded as another Siberia, fit only for malefactors and libertines, and standards of competence and morality were usually low, except sometimes in the higher appointments. Moreover, Europeans were particularly liable to be put out of action by intestinal disorders, malaria, or yellow fever, diseases which might well be made worse when treated by the methods of contemporary European medicine, but to which African populations might acquire early immunity. So the French began to take Africans on to their payroll in increasing numbers. Some, locally known as *laptots,* worked as unskilled laborers or as river boatmen, who often had to pull the vessels along by ropes from the bank, and most of them were recruited as required from neighboring Wolof states; they were not necessarily permanent residents in the settlements, and might be dismissed as doubtfully loyal when France was in dispute with Walo or Cayor. But even in the seventeenth century free Negroes were permanently employed as specialist tradesmen —carpenters, coopers, smiths, masons, bakers—and as interpreters and captains of riverboats.[7]

From the status of salaried employees, some Africans moved into commerce on their own account. For most of the eighteenth and some of the nineteenth centuries the foreign trade of Saint-Louis was legally monopolized by French companies, but their African agents were often shrewd and skillful in exploiting their opportunities within the colonial commerce. Since the annual trading voyages to the gum *escales* and to Galam were always uncomfortable, and often unhealthy and hazardous, Frenchmen tended increasingly to leave them to Senegalese traders. In 1785 only one Frenchman, Saugnier, made

[7] For detailed references to the following pages, see *JAH* VI (1965), 177-84, where a slightly different version appears under the title "Assimilation in Eighteenth Century Senegal." I am grateful to the editors for permission to reprint this passage. In revising it I have been able to use two more recent articles: Léonce Joure, "Les établissements sur la Côte occidentale de l'Afrique de 1758 à 1809," *Revue française de l'histoire d'Outre-mer,* LI (1964); and Françoise Deroure, "La vie Quotidienne à Saint Louis par ses Archives, 1779-1809," *Bulletin de l'IFAN,* series B, xxvi (1964), 397-439.

the trip to Galam, and he noted three different types of relationships between the African traders and their European backers. Some traders were given merchandise on credit and bound themselves to deliver one slave for each 120 or 130 "bars"; others undertook to buy slaves at 100 bars apiece, but carried no responsibility if their purchases escaped or died before they were delivered to the merchants in Saint-Louis; a few were sent on a profit-sharing basis in charge of vessels fitted out directly by Frenchmen. None of these systems seemed satisfactory to Saugnier; "all the faults and all the misfortunes fall upon the whites, and all the profit goes to the negroes." But credit in any of these forms might serve to lay the foundations of a modest Senegalese family fortune. And as French trade developed in the southern rivers, similar opportunities seem to have opened before African inhabitants of Gorée.

The third method by which the Senegalese community expanded was through interracial marriage and concubinage. Since white women were virtually unknown in the eighteenth century, mulatto children soon began to appear. Some French authorities in Senegal (though not their superiors in France) were glad to encourage interracial *ménages* as likely to produce a more stable community; Frenchmen provided with home comforts were less likely to desert and set up as private traders. So, when marriage according to Catholic rites was not possible or expedient, unions *à la mode du pays* were celebrated with some formality, constituting family relationships of recognized status which often endured happily until the man returned to Europe. Paternity of mulatto offspring, it has been noted, was almost invariably acknowledged in the colonial registers.[8] These children were usually educated, sometimes in France, and provided with career opportunities within the settlement. Their mothers also acquired something of the wealth and social status of their consorts; *signarees,* as these often formidable women were called, acquired property, entered trade, and became respected members of the community. In 1786 Governor de Boufflers, an aristocratic litterateur, gave a ball for the ladies of Gorée; it is doubtful whether any of them had been born in Europe.

The fourth element was recently evoked by President Senghor's remark that many Senegalese speak Portuguese Creole as their mother tongue. At several points along the coast south of Cape Verde— notably at Joal, where Abbé Demanet claimed to find eight hundred

[8] Deroure, *op. cit.,* p. 409.

people awaiting the opportunity of baptism in 1764—there long remained remnants of Portuguese influence in the shape of traders and others who took Portuguese names and observed residuary practices of Christianity. Through their dealing with French priests and traders, in time some of these relics of an earlier colonial enterprise became merged in the Senegalese community.

This community was still quite small. Estimates of the 1770s suggest that between twelve and fifteen hundred free Negroes and mulattoes lived in Saint-Louis, and perhaps 250 at Gorée. To these may be added two hundred or so Europeans, and a tiny community of Moroccans, who maintained the old links across the desert with Fez. The total population of Saint-Louis however was three or four thousand; soon after the French reoccupation it was said to have risen to five or six thousand, by the end of the century to nearly ten thousand. The growth was largely due to the increasing number of captives withdrawn from the commercial slave market for domestic service, general labor, or military service. The majority of these were Bambaras; they had a good reputation for hard work and docility, and since their homeland was several hundred miles away they were unlikely to abscond. These household slaves were rarely sold abroad, unless they committed a crime or their owners went bankrupt; prosperous Senegalese, unable to invest their savings in foreign commerce, bought slaves to serve them on future trading voyages, or to embellish their households in Saint-Louis. These captives became part of the Senegalese community, and experienced some of the effects of the process of assimilation which was now going on.

What did this assimilation mean? In the first place, it meant the profession of the Catholic faith, the religion of all Frenchmen and so, in principle, of the inhabitants of French settlements overseas. But although instructions from French Companies and Ministers repeatedly expressed concern to further the conversion of their African subjects and employees, this was not always supported by practical provisions. For substantial periods no priests resided in Senegal, and those who did so were often not particularly spiritual men; no separate Church building was begun until 1827, and the sacraments were celebrated in a room in the chaplain's house; there is no record of schools maintained in the eighteenth century by Church, state, or Companies. In these circumstances, it is remarkable that so many of them not only became practicing Catholics but retained their alle-

giance when deprived of resident clergy over prolonged periods—
notably during the British occupations of Saint-Louis (1758-78, 1809-
17) and Gorée (1759-63, 1779-83, 1800-17). Although the terms on
which the French surrendered Saint-Louis in 1758 stipulated that
mulattoes and free Negroes would not be molested in their religion,
British governors apparently attempted to convert them to Protestant-
ism; but without success. The Catholic community continued to meet
for worship under the leadership of Charles Thevenot, a mulatto of
good education and wide influence; the Epistle and Gospel would be
read and parts of the Office sung.[9] In 1776 Governor McNamara appealed for Protestant clergy and teachers to stop "the vile custom of
going to Gorée daily for confession and marriage," and lamented that
after eighteen years of British occupation "the Children of the English, even of my Council, are breeding up to the Popish faith." During
the period of priestless French rule which followed the Revolution,
the Catholic Senegalese gathered regularly for prayer in the former
chapel. The constancy of the Senegalese Catholics is far more impressive than the missionary effort put out toward them by the French
Church.

But not all French subjects became assimilated in religion. It was
inevitable that Saint-Louis and Gorée, drawing immigrants from sur-
rounding countries of more or less loyal Muslim allegiance, should
also contain a sizeable Muslim population. Many were domestic
slaves (and the custom which developed in Saint-Louis of liberating
those who were converted to Christianity may have inhibited the evan-
gelistic zeal of their masters), but free Muslim traders also resided
and visited there. Adanson's account of the enthusiastic public celebrations of *Tabaski* in the 1750s suggests that the Saint-Louis Muslim
community was numerous and conspicuous. Their contacts with African Catholics produced examples of what modern anthropologists
would describe as syncretism. In 1789 Lamiral noted among Saint-
Louis Christians "a curious admixture of Mohammedism and idol-
atry." They would celebrate both Christian and Muslim festivals,
make the *salaam* as well as attend Mass, and pray with equal fervor
to Christ and Muhammed. A devout Christian mulatto woman might
rejoice with the Muslims on the appearance of the new moon, alter-

[9] Joure, *op. cit.*, pp. 411-2, quotes an account of the service in 1775; see also
John Lindsay, A *Voyage to the Coast of Africa in 1758* (London, 1759), pp.
75-80.

nately prostrating and crossing herself in thanksgiving. Gorée, isolated on its island, may have been slightly more orthodox; but even here marriage ceremonies were influenced by Wolof customs, themselves more animist than Muslim. From the seventeenth century European visitors were surprised to see *griots* participating in Christian weddings, performing crude rituals designed to attest the bride's virginity. The Catholicism of the Senegalese showed in its outward observances clear traces of the African cultural environment; its flexibility may in part explain its strength.

Secondly, assimilation involved the limited introduction into the Senegalese community of European-type institutions. The earliest civic duty of the *habitants* was that of bearing arms in defense of the settlement. Although there was no regularly constituted African auxiliary force until 1818, as early as 1685 la Courbe was prepared to rely on the loyalty of Christian Negroes in a dispute with Walo, and in 1758 the French armed 1500 of them to assist in defending Saint-Louis against the British. The British in turn were prepared to rely on Senegalese Christians for defense against neighboring Africans, though not against France. Meanwhile in civil government the French, finding it expedient to refer minor criminal offences and administrative problems to an accredited spokesman of the community, had already begun to nominate a leading *habitant* as Mayor in each of their towns.[10] At Saint-Louis Charles Thevenot maintained his position and represented the interests of the community during the British occupation of the 1760s. When the French Crown took over in 1778 it provided salaries for the Mayors, of 1200 livres per annum at Saint-Louis and 720 at Gorée.[11]

There also seems to have been some development of judicial arrangements. Instructions to the first Royal Governor assumed that he would be able to maintain "good order and tranquility" by a sort of paternal rough justice, administered where appropriate with the collaboration of senior military officers. But the exercise of this vice-regal authority was in practice controlled by customary usage, which took account of the rights of the *habitants*. According to Durand, capital charges were in the mid-1780s tried by the Governor in the presence

[10] Joure, *op. cit.*, p. 257.
[11] For an account of the diversity of the Mayor's duties, see P. Alquier, "Saint-Louis du Sénégal sous la Révolution et l'Empire," *BCEHSAOF*, V (1922), 277-320, 411-63.

of a number of officials, including the Mayor. Africans, if convicted, were not executed but sold to the West Indies (and part of the price given to the injured party); Europeans who had injured *habitants* could be sent back to France. In civil cases the Governor would sit with three assessors, of the same color as the parties; in interracial cases, with assessors of both colors. It might be argued that the civil rights of the Senegalese in the 1780s were more clearly recognized than those of some of their French contemporaries.[12]

Thirdly, assimilation meant that some Senegalese consciously accepted standards and values derived from their European rulers, and in return claimed the rights which they believed such acceptance should bring. When Saint-Louis surrendered in 1758, the Company stipulated, and the British agreed, that free Negroes and mulattoes of both sexes should remain at liberty, should retain their property, and should not be persecuted in their religion. When these undertakings were not satisfactorily carried out, the Senegalese resorted to constitutional protest. In 1759 a petition, drafted in French, complained that African property was being commandeered for officers' quarters; it was signed by sixteen men, including Thevenot as Mayor, and twenty-six other *habitants et habitantes chrétiennes* added their marks. Under the long governorship of Colonel O'Hara the *habitants* were apparently compelled to suffer in silence; but in January 1776 a whole series of complaints, from both men and women, was presented before his successor in Council, and in a formal petition written in very adequate English. It was alleged that O'Hara had sold free Africans into slavery, had confiscated houses for the use of colleagues and concubines, and generally used arbitrary proceedings and abusive language. To the latter, one formidable *signaree* had retorted that "tho her skin was black, her heart was white and her blood as good as his"; it is evident that an element of racial consciousness already reinforced this determination to defend the rights of the community. The returning French, though welcomed as kinsmen, soon discovered that Senegalese loyalty did not imply subservience. Whereas instructions to the Governor in 1782 referred to the African Christians in complimentary terms, those of the following year used such terms as "vicious" and "idleness," suggesting that the authorities had detected an unwelcome spirit of independence.

[12] There may be room for research, however, on how justice was actually rendered in practice; cf. Alquier, *op. cit.*, pp. 453-59.

The influence of European culture on Senegalese society is more easily discernible than the African contributions. Sociologists studying modern African towns have shown how African immigrants commonly form voluntary associations with their countrymen for purposes of mutual assistance and recreation; such a society for Wolof women, the *mbotaye*, was described by Boilat in 1853, and it had clearly existed much earlier. It would be interesting to know how far such communities of Wolof or other immigrants constituted channels of communications between the settlements and the neighboring peoples: how far the *maîtres de langues* employed by the French translated cultures as well as languages. Modern analogies again suggest that there is often a network of family and other relationships between colonial towns and the countryside around, and there is some evidence that this was also so in eighteenth-century Senegal. The *Compagnie des Indes* tried to discourage interracial marriage for fear that its servants would trade with their in-laws at the expense of the Company's interests; the British, after taking Gorée in 1759, discovered that the leading inhabitants were so closely "allied to the principal people on the Continent" that they had to be conciliated if the garrison was to obtain supplies of water, wood, and provisions from Cayor or Sine. It is difficult to say how closely or for how many generations such bonds were maintained; but in so far as the *habitant* community recruited new members by immigration, they were presumably renewed from time to time.

It nevertheless does not appear that French policy was very successful in harmonizing the interests of the *habitants* with those of the Wolofs, Fulas, and Trarzas of the lower Senegal valley. The interaction of French trade and African politics in the eighteenth century is a subject which still awaits its historian; when he comes to examine his French sources he will find they often record incomprehension, and inconsistency. Although a few Frenchmen observed African cultures with care and sympathy—a dictionary of the Wolof language was published in the 1790s—officials generally showed an ethnocentric intolerance which did not facilitate the adjustment of disputes. The continuance of the commerce which was the sole reason for the French presence depended on the reciprocal interests of her African customers, stimulated by the payment of customary duties to the authorities responsible for the ordering of the markets. Africans referred to these payments by terms used to describe the tax which

Muslim rulers required their Christian subjects to pay; its translation as "tribute" reflected a situation in which European traders remained ultimately dependent on the tolerance of their African neighbors. No French governor ever succeeded in constituting a durable system of political alliances; their settlements simply became one more unit in the complex pattern of inter-African relations, better armed than the others perhaps, but weaker in manpower and in knowledge of the country.

Changes in European Attitudes

Toward the end of the eighteenth century there were signs of change, not so much in French Senegalese policy as over the whole field of European attitudes toward Africa. It is difficult to isolate any single fundamental reason for this; new approaches to the continent intersected in a complex manner. These included a new interest in finding markets for European manufactures by trade with the interior of Africa; a great extension of intellectual curiosity about the physical and human geography of the continent (mostly known, if at all, only through Leo Africanus or earlier writers), and a growing humanitarian concern about the future destiny of its peoples, leading eventually to public questioning of the legitimacy of the slave trade. Together the new ideas pointed toward a conclusion which, obvious though it may now seem, was revolutionary in its implications: that African labor might be used to produce a wider range of products within Africa itself. Senegal might be regarded as the home of this idea. Chambonneau in 1693 seems to have thought primarily of introducing European farmers; but from the time of the Seven Years War Frenchmen began to argue with increasing vigor in favor of promoting the cultivation by African farmers of such crops as indigo, sugar, and cotton, which would otherwise have to be obtained from the American tropics. Senegal, the Bissagos Islands, the Saloum and Casamance valleys, were areas particularly favored for such projects.[18] Similar ideas occurred to the British. Senegal, annexed in 1763, was united with the Gambia settlements in a new Crown Colony called Senegambia; Governor O'Hara had high hopes for its future. Enthusiastically taking up ideas already adumbrated

[18] Delcourt, op. cit., p. 83; Joure, op. cit., pp. 349-76. J. B. Demanet, Nouvelle histoire de l'Afrique Françoise, two vols. (Paris, 1767), see also Roger Mercier, L'Afrique Noire dans la Littérature française (Dakar, 1962), Chapters V and VI.

by a naval officer, John Lindsay, O'Hara wrote of developing the gold
trade with Bambouk, promoting European settlement in Galam and
the cultivation of rice, cotton, tobacco, and indigo, and of establishing
trade with Sudanese markets still served only through the Sahara.
Beyond the mines, Europeans were beginning to perceive the fascinat-
ing mirage of a vast trade with Timbuktu.[14]

American independence provided additional reasons for Europeans
to reconsider the basis of their relations with the world overseas.
After recovering Senegal in 1779 the French monarchy groped its
way toward a more active policy, especially on more southerly coasts.
For the first time, French ships began to show interest in the coasts
of modern Guinea, and more specifically in the Isles de Los. In 1785
a small fort was established for the benefit of French traders on
Gambia Island in the Sierra Leone estuary. On the Gold Coast,
where French traders had been at a disadvantage since the British
excluded them from Anomabu in midcentury, a post was established
at Amoku in 1786; next year a Treaty (which in the end was not
followed up) provided for another shore establishment at Lahou on
the Ivory Coast. The Royal Governor of Whydah was assigned a
more active role in protecting and developing French commerce
between the Ivory Coast and Allada; since the value of the local
slave trade was declining, the French fort was to be developed as
the Gorée of the Bights.[15] Further east still Captain Landolphe, a
picturesque individualist from St. Malo, established a footing in
Warri, whence he shipped to France the first samples of palm oil
(but he could only envisage its domestic use, not yet its industrial
exploitation).[16] These were interesting new departures, but they
hardly amount to a new African policy. In Senegal itself affairs became increasingly dominated by another company, which in the face
of local antagonism sought privileges for the pursuit of familiar
objectives—the control of the gum trade, the development of commerce in Galam, the supply of slaves to new French plantations in
Guyana. Although some Frenchmen were beginning to appreciate

[14] PRO. C.O. 267/13, O'Hara to Conway, May 28, July 25, Sept. 1, 1766. *Cf.*
Lindsay, *op. cit.*, pp. 94-107; also A *Plea for Improving the Trade at Senegal,
addressed to the Lords Commissioners for Trade and Plantations* (London,
1763).
    [15] Instructions to Gourg, Nov. 23, 1786, in Schefer, *Instructions Générales*
I (Paris, 1921), pp. 216-22. More generally, see Labarthe, *op. cit.*
    [16] J. S. Quesne (ed.), *Mémoires du Capitaine Landolphe* (Paris, 1823), I, 99n.

The effects of the French Revolution in Africa still await thorough
study. It might have been expected that action against slavery would
be taken by the revolutionaries, in sympathy with the movement to
illegalize the slave trade which was gathering force in Great Britain.
Historians have differed in their assessment of the British Abolitionists, and the debate extends too widely to be summed up here;[18]
but most would now agree that the moral fervor which inspired Clark-
son and Wilberforce would not have made so strong or rapid an impact had not the British economy already begun to be less dependent
than formerly on the Atlantic plantation economy. Their conviction
that the slave traffic was an affront to human dignity could thus be
reinforced by arguments tending to show that it might also represent
an uneconomical use of African resources. But in France, although
the Société des Amis des Noirs, also founded in 1788, commanded
respect through the intellectual distinction and enlightenment of
members such as Condorcet, Mirabeau, Sièyes, Lafayette, Brissot,
the social and political conditions which enabled the English Evan-
gelicals to mount one of the first modern political campaigns were
lacking. Moreover, it seemed to some Frenchmen that Britain would
be the chief gainer if the undeveloped plantations of Saint-Domingue
were prevented from recruiting slave labor. Even if the spirit of 1789
was hard to reconcile with slavery, slave-owners were present in the
revolutionary assemblies to make the attempt; and the development
of legislation and policy on this question was determined by West
Indian rather than African needs and interests. Not until May 1794
was slavery legally abolished in the French colonies, and even this
proved only a temporary change, with little effect on Africa.

[17] On this see J. Machat, Documents sur les Etablissements français (Paris,
1921), esp. the memoirs of c. 1772 and 1783 on pp. 115-8, 135-6.
[18] Compare Reginald Coupland, Wilberforce (London, 1923) and The British
Anti-Slavery Movement (London, 1933) with Eric Williams, Capitalism and
Slavery (Chapel Hill, 1944). My own views are indicated in The New Cambridge
Modern History, Vol. VIII (Cambridge, 1965), pp. 247-51. On France see
Gaston-Martin, Histoire de l'Esclavage dans les Colonies françaises (Paris, 1948).

Unlike France's West and East Indian colonies, Senegal was not represented in the Revolutionary assemblies. It was nevertheless affected by the revolutionary spirit. In April 1789 a meeting of *habitants* of all races under the mulatto mayor, Charles Cornier, drafted a *cahier* calling on the Estates-General to abolish the commercial monopoly of the Senegal Company: "an odious privilege, equally contrary to the laws of reason and of nature, which by violating the law of nations destroys the foundations of wise policy." The immediate effects of the Revolution included some practical extensions of the rights of the *habitants*; they were assembled to discuss certain decisions and hear news of great events in Europe; there was for a time an elected Colonial Council, a volunteer force with elected officers. French Jacobinism seems to have found sympathetic echoes in Senegal; in August 1794 a deputation claiming to represent the inhabitants of all colors made a patriotic gift to the Convention of over 20,000 *livres*. It is doubtful however whether the Emancipation Act of 1794 made any difference to the position of domestic slaves in *habitant* households; it is certain that the growing stream of African immigrants into the impoverished colony were not welcomed into citizenship.[19]

For economically, the war was disastrous for the French African settlements. From 1793 their foreign trade and communications were cut off by British naval power; the government of Senegal remained chronically short of cash and food supplies. At Whydah the tiny garrison, harassed by social and political upheavals in Dahomey as well as by the interruption of trade, was affected even more drastically and withdrew in 1797. In Senegal the popular Governor Blanchot maintained his position largely by benevolent authoritarianism; his successor Laserre, accused of reviving monopoly to his personal advantage, lost the confidence of his subjects. In July 1802 a rising of the African and mulatto population removed him from office, with belated cries of "Vive la Convention! Vive Robespierre!" and 27 Negro and mulatto *habitants* signed a manifesto against his "arbitrary and despotic acts." [20]

As Napoleon consolidated his personal power in France, authoritarian trends in colonial policy increased. Slavery again became legal

---

[19] Dominique Harcourt Lamiral, *L'Affrique et le Peuple Affriquain* (Paris, 1789), pp. 1-40; Alquier, *op. cit., passim.*

[20] Cultru, *op. cit.,* pp. 287-89; Joure, *op. cit.,* especially pp. 164-73, 432-25.

in May 1802, and new restrictions were placed on the immigration into France of colored people. Following the insurrection of 1802 the position of *habitants* in the Senegalese defense force was re-examined, and Blanchot warned to maintain distinctions of color.[21] Napoleon's Egyptian expedition had shown his interest in the African continent, and some attention was now given in Paris to schemes for exploration. These were no doubt seen as rejoinders to the achievements of the British African Association—although such were the international decencies of the period that representatives of that Association received cordial cooperation from the French authorities when they needed it.[22] But the British occupation of Saint-Louis in 1809 removed any possibility of a new African policy under the Empire. France recovered her Senegalese settlements in 1817 without any very clear idea about their future development. However, the international situation had been changed by the growth of anti-slavery movements; and, more mildly, the atmosphere in Senegal had been changed by a whiff of Jacobinism. It would not be possible for France to go on in Africa as before.

[21] Schefer, *op. cit.*, Vol. I, p. 189, Memoir for Blanchot, 29 Thermidor an X; Joure, *op. cit.*, pp. 208-20.

[22] Robin Hallett (ed.), *Records of the African Association, 1788-1831* (London, 1964), pp. 180-260.

SIX

THE NINETEENTH-CENTURY TRANSITION

When the European powers made peace after the Napole-onic Wars they were little concerned about African territory. Britain did not want to accumulate colonies which served no clear purpose in her new and largely economic imperial strategy; the Cape of Good Hope was one exception, but her Senegalese conquests were not. The Treaty of Paris of 1814 therefore aimed to restore the territorial and commercial interests of Britain and France in West Africa to the position of 1783. The main effects on Africa came from a different feature of the postwar settlement. Since 1808 British Abolitionists, having succeeded in making the slave trade illegal for British subjects, had urged their government to constrain other nations to do so; they were now vigorously if incongruously sup-ported by the West Indian lobby, anxious that the plantation hands they were now forbidden to import should not be used to develop the virgin lands of Cuba and Brazil. In 1815 the twice-restored French monarchy agreed to forbid its subjects to trade in slaves; and British diplomatists and naval officers embarked on prolonged efforts to compel foreign governments and traders, European and African, to do likewise.

The effects of abolition on African economic, political, and social structures provides the principal theme of the history of the West African coast during the next fifty years. These effects were felt un-evenly, at speeds largely determined by European initiatives. As it had been a European idea to start exporting African slaves across the Atlantic, so it was a European idea to forbid this. Africans, puzzled by the mutable morality of their white customers, did not all respond immediately or enthusiastically. Failing the presence on a particular coast of merchants ready to buy alternative produce, it was difficult to respond at all. Until the early 1860s slavers were the most active traders in many districts; increasing demands for labor in Brazil, Cuba, and the southern U.S.A., raised slave prices, tempted dealers to trade in defiance of the British naval patrols, and made it more profitable for many Africans to continue to satisfy this demand than to experiment with new cash-crops. By the 1830s, palm oil provided a profitable alternative staple in some areas, notably the Niger delta; where there was no such ready substitute for slaves, naval coercion might be needed to suppress trade in them. During the period 1815-80, therefore, the development of the coastal regions was increasingly influenced by European actions; the shape of future colonies began to impose itself on the complex mosaic of African politics.

In Senegambia, where the economy had never depended completely on slaving and European forts already controlled the rivers, suppression of the export trade was relatively speedy, although official French policies of buying slaves to enroll as soldiers, or to send across the ocean as freely indentured laborers, provided a continuing stimulus to internal dealings in men. But the development of an alternative economy was much slower. Saint-Louis and Gorée, with populations now around 10,000 and 5,000,[1] had lost a sizeable sector of their prewar business; the restored French monarchy tried to compensate by sponsoring experiments in agricultural colonization on lines foreshadowed in the eighteenth century. Their first governor, Colonel Julien Schmaltz, had served in Java, and admired the methods by which the Dutch tried to combine the maintenance of indigenous rulers with the exploitation of agricultural resources. In the Senegal valley he planned to secure the cession of lands which could be let out to ex-servicemen, European investors, or enterprising *habitants* (to whom he was prepared to advance part of the 5,000 francs estimated as necessary working capital for a small farm).[2] But land could only be obtained through the cooperation of some neighboring

---

[1] From the mid-1820s detailed official estimates of population, though not all classified in comparable categories, appear in the *Annales Maritimes et Coloniales*. The figures for January 1, 1826 are:

	Blancs	Hommes de couleur et Noirs affranchis	Aborigènes libres	Captifs	Totals
Saint-Louis	220	642	1,475	7,968	10,305
Gorée	40	713	743	4,329	5,825
Total	260	1,355	2,218	12,297	16,130

[2] Schefer, *op. cit.*, Vol. I, pp. 280-310, Instructions to Schmaltz, Dec. 31, 1818.

African ruler; and close collaboration with any one was liable to earn France the hostility of others. Schmaltz looked first to the Tokolors of Futa Toro and supplied them with firearms to use against the Bambaras; their state lay in one of the more fertile parts of the valley, it dominated the river trade, and its theocratic institutions seemed to prepare the way for civilization as Schmaltz understood it. But it was also distinguished by a complex political structure, internal social and theological divisions (which Al Hajj 'Umar was later to exploit) and some unsatisfactory experiences of dealing with the French. In 1819 Schmaltz, despairing of quick agreement with Futa Toro, switched his plans suddenly and secured rights to less fertile lands, nearer to Saint-Louis, from the Wolof state of Walo. The consequence, as often when inexperienced governors attempted a political coup, was disastrous; Futa Toro joined other enemies of Walo—Cayor and the Trarza Moors—in an alliance prejudicial not only to agricultural projects but to the river trade.

This hostility was temporarily appeased by Schmaltz's successor, Baron Roger (1822-27) who convinced his neighbors that he would respect their sovereignty and interfere less in their internal affairs. Roger, formerly manager of the Crown domain in the colony, made a remarkably intensive attempt to apply agronomic science to the development of Walo. An experimental farm under the French "gardener" Richard attempted to acclimatize a wide range of European and tropical exotic crops, studying with particular care the problems of developing cotton and indigo. Experiments were made to determine methods of irrigation and ploughing, of cotton-ginning and indigo preparation, which could be applied in Senegalese conditions. Eminent scientists in Paris, including Gay-Lussac, were asked to analyze specimens of Senegalese plants and soils; less eminent chemists went out to Africa in person. In Saint-Louis Roger sponsored an Agricultural Society, a library, and agricultural exhibitions; he hoped thus to spread more scientific methods first to colonial, eventually to African, farmers. In Walo he granted nearly fifty concessions of unoccupied land to Europeans and *habitants*; he provided a generous system of bounties and prizes for cotton and indigo, to be available for Wolof producers also. No comparable attempt to encourage economic development by comprehensive governmental action would be made until the twentieth century.[3]

[3] For these experiments, the essential work is Georges Hardy, *La Mise en Valeur du Sénégal de 1817 à 1854* (Paris, 1921).

Yet by 1831 little trace was left of Roger's work, except the vegetable garden of Richard-Toll. Some of Roger's miscalculations arose from faulty assessment of the people through whom he would have to work. Few of the European merchants or Senegalese *habitants* who took up concessions in Walo were really prepared to invest much capital or personal effort in attempts to raise and control a labor force capable of applying scientific methods to the barren soil of Walo; the subsidies offered induced some to make token efforts, others to engage in fraud.[4] Another limitation was imposed by France's protectionist colonial policy; cotton and indigo were chosen as the crops to be developed, not as a result of study of local potentialities, but because the French economy needed them. Though varieties of both plants grew in the Senegal valley, the scientists of the period (who reported on their chemical analyses of soils with insufficient regard to effects of a tropical environment) were overoptimistic in their hopes of developing cultivation of these crops at economic prices. Senegalese indigo was not only inferior to Bengali varieties, but much more expensive; Senegalese cotton only once began seriously to enter world markets, when the shortage of supplies during the American Civil War allowed the colonial government to offer attractive guaranteed prices to African producers.[5] In this case, as in so many others, world market conditions imposed severe restrictions on the possibilities of African economic development.

After the liquidation of Roger's colonization schemes, the economy of Saint-Louis became more dependent on the gum trade than ever before. An increased population struggled to earn a living at a period when the development of chemical substitutes and increased competition from Egyptian gum were depressing world prices. Ventures into African politics by inexperienced Governors brought more problems than advantages. A marriage alliance between Walo and the Trarzas enclosed Saint-Louis in a tight ring of formidable and exacting neighbors. While Frenchmen and Senegalese competed with stereotyped methods to purchase limited quantities of gum at the *escales,* and argued about the respective merits of free competition and protective regulation, their Moorish suppliers were enabled to raise their prices, and their demands for those customary payments still described as "tribute."

[4] Anne Raffenel, V*oyage dans l'Afrique occidentale* (Paris, 1846), pp. 21-3.

[5] Roger Pasquier, "Les Essais de Culture du Coton au Sénégal," *Annales Africaines* (Dakar, 1955).

In the 1830s a few merchants began to realize the economic possibilities of the groundnut (or peanut), which had been cultivated by Africans in coastal districts north of Sierra Leone for three centuries. Some Frenchmen proposed to express oil locally for export to France, and asked for official encouragement. But the French government was anxious to protect olive oil producers of the Midi from competition, and refused this opportunity to promote Senegal's first export industry. However, they reduced the duty on unprocessed groundnuts; and despite heavy transport costs, Senegal was, by 1852, sending nearly 3,000 tons of these to France. Thus began the exploitation of Senegal's major cash crop, which did not require government colonization schemes or the alienation of African land to settlers. But the cultivation and marketing of groundnuts on any really extensive scale would require stable political conditions in the Senegambia region; and France still possessed neither the power nor the political skill to provide them.

Failure to find a new basis for the Senegalese economy left the *habitant* community of Saint-Louis in a condition of arrested development. Excluded from participating directly in overseas trade, they reflected the commercial conservatism of the French merchants on whose capital they depended. *Habitants* still conducted the river trade and assumed civil and military responsibilities in unhealthy outposts like Bakel; some, like Paul Holle, greatly distinguished themselves in these spheres. But any chances of making a fortune in the gum trade were receding; and political and financial obstacles inhibited residents of Saint-Louis from prosperity. In contemporary Sierra Leone and Liberia, African communities partly assimilated to the values of western society were doing much to advance the colonial frontiers of "Christianity, civilization, and commerce"; but in the Senegal valley, these frontiers remained essentially where they had been in the eighteenth century.

Some traces of French influence were carried toward the Sudan by former slaves from Saint-Louis. Domestic slavery was not immediately affected by the ban on exports, and the government, like private individuals, still recruited laborers, soldiers, and servants for fixed terms of up to fourteen years. They were then free to return to their homelands. A French expedition to Bondou in 1833-44 met a former hospital orderly there, and contacts with such men may have influenced the readiness of the Alimani to offer incentives to French trad-ers.[6] After slavery was legally ended in Saint-Louis and Gorée in 1848, although most of those liberated continued in their former employ-ment, there was more migration of Muslims to the interior; Al Hajj 'Umar, as already noted, benefited by recruiting craftsmen as *talibés*. Although French influence upon these men was clearly limited, it should not be wholly discounted: witness the French traveller to Ségou in 1878 who was hailed by a shout of "Liberté. Mil huit cent quarante-huit! Merci!"[7] But on the whole, the influence of Saint-Louis expanded only slowly.

To Governor Roger in 1826, the community of Gorée—"soft, indo-lent, and poor to boot"—seemed even less capable of becoming a growing point of French influence.[8] During the war British occupation had brought some prosperity, based on trade with the southern coast and rivers; this declined when the French returned, and leading citi-zens of both sexes migrated to British Gambia. But the French made some attempts to compensate by fiscal policies designed to encourage the use of the island as an *entrepôt*, and gradually Goréen trade and influence spread into the small African states of the southern rivers. In the Casamance region, posts were set up in the 1830s to encourage political as well as commercial competition with the Portuguese, and the support of French power ensured that this valley was eventually attached to the Senegalese sphere of influence. But there was a much greater development of French groundnut trade in the Gambia valley, where British influence predominated; here France indeed gave up Albreda in 1857.

In the estuaries of modern Guinea illicit exports of slaves contin-ued until about 1865, in competition with trade in locally grown produce and gold and hides brought down from Futa Jalon. Coastal traders and commission agents based on Gorée took longer to com-pete with those of Sierra Leone, and missionary activity long re-mained confined to English-speaking Protestants. But gradually French influence was introduced, by naval visits and later by traders, and this led to proposals of political intervention. In 1829 a naval

[6] Françoise Deroure, "La Vie quotidienne à Saint Louis," *loc. cit.*, 1966, pp. 415-16. F. Zuccarelli, "Le régime des engagés à temps au Sénégal, 1817-48, *CEA* No. 7 (1962). Raffenel, *op. cit.*, pp. 158, 122-24.

[7] Paul Soleillet, *Voyage à Ségou* (Paris, 1887), p. 393.

[8] Hardy, *op. cit.*, pp. 219-20.

officer suggested establishing a fortified trading post in the river Pongos;[9] in 1839 the first of a series of treaties gave France an interest in the complicated politics of the Nunez. The July monarchy gave little support to such local initiatives, refusing even to encourage the importation of Nunez coffee by taxing it as if grown on French colonial soil; but after 1848 the growing demand for groundnuts provided some merchants of Gorée with opportunities to develop their trade in Guinea, as well as nearer home. But even now few French merchants showed much enterprise on the more distant coasts, and they did not invariably seek direct political control by their government. African traders and rulers could still to a large degree decide how to respond to their presence.

The Senegalese Community

Despite their limited economic opportunities, Senegalese residents of African descent continued to enjoy certain educational opportunities and civic rights. The educational opportunities were rather makeshift. Before the revolution Frenchmen provided education for their mulatto offspring either by sending them to France or by improvised arrangements for their instruction by French soldiers or servants of the Company. The need for trading auxiliaries and artisans meant that selected Africans also might receive some improvised vocational training. During the nineteenth century those provisions were supplemented only slowly. The European churches did not undertake, as they did at Sierra Leone, the task of training African agents for the conversion of their continent; throughout the century missions made little headway in Senegal in face of the appeal of Islam and its traditional Koranic schools. In the colonial towns the government gradually undertook to provide schools for the children of the *habitants* and such African children as could benefit from them; but progress was slow. There were sectarian rivalries among the various Orders charged with the work; there were difficulties in recruiting suitable teachers and in adapting the syllabus to African conditions. (There seems to have been general approval for teaching primary-school children about the Merovingian dynasty and the bishoprics of France, but one Apostolic Prefect did object to including Indian mythology in the sylla-

[9] *Annales Maritimes et Coloniales*, 1830, Pt. II, Tome II, pp. 116-27 (Report by C.A.D.).

bus.)[10] In 1829 it was decided to replace Wolof by French as the medium of elementary instruction. This important decision did not entirely succeed in its purpose of replacing African cultural influences by French (since, to the despair of the Fathers, even mulatto children were still addressed by their mothers in their native Wolof, and thereby taught "superstitious ideas, obscene songs, and stories")[11]; but it inhibited the progress of all but the most adaptable African children. Attempts to provide secondary education locally for the minority (largely mulatto) who mastered the primary syllabus were even less successful. Many *habitants* preferred the government to provide their children with scholarships for study in France; but the results were frequently discouraging. Some children deteriorated in health and died; others, the authorities feared, acquired disturbing and subversive ideas.

Despite these complaints, a trickle of Senegalese children acquired sufficient learning to give satisfactory, sometimes distinguished, service to the government, the commercial companies, more rarely the Church. There were experiments in technical education, and later in the century schools were even opened in such interior villages as Podor, and Sedhiou in Casamance. But numbers were small. Even in 1883, when a start had been made with secular education intended to appeal to Muslims, only just over a thousand pupils were receiving full-time education in the colony, although evening classes, an increasingly popular form of education for those outside the elite, had nearly six hundred pupils.[12] Only eleven children were receiving post-primary education in Senegal; so long as the *habitants* could send children to train in France or Algeria with government scholarships there was little demand from below to develop local facilities for higher study.

In civic affairs the rights of *habitants* were becoming linked with those of Frenchmen; the July monarchy explicitly confirmed the prin-

[10] Archives AAOF, J 1., Report by Arbalosse, 1846; cf. report on schools of Gorée, Sept. 6, 1850. Mlle. Denise Bouche of the University of Dakar is studying the history of Senegalese education; meanwhile consult Georges Hardy, "L'enseignement au Sénégal de 1817 à 1854," BCEHSAOF, IV (1921). For an indication of the new approach of the Holy Ghost Fathers at Dakar after 1845 see Note of Laprade, Nov. 13, 1857, Charpy, *La Fondation de Dakar* (Paris, 1958), pp. 20, 45.

[11] AAOF J 1., Report by Maynard, Sept. 20, 1842.

[12] G. Haurigot, *Le Sénégal* (Paris, 1887), pp. 178-82.

ciple that all free residents of French colonies could enjoy civic and political rights as prescribed by law. The oligarchical constitution of France thus cast a shadow into Africa. "Respectable" Senegalese of all races joined in pressing for such concrete measures as the establishment of local Chambers of Commerce, improvements in postal, customs, and pilot services, the creation of local credit institutions. Habitants were represented on the governor's conseil d'administration, served on various advisory commissions, continued to be appointed as Mayors. Between 1840 and 1848 there was an active and articulate conseil-général at Saint-Louis, consisting of four European and four "native" members, plus two retail traders who could be of any race. They were elected through an "assembly of notable habitants and officials," nominated by the governor so that about half its members were Europeans. A conseil d'administration at Gorée was constituted in a similar way.[13] The majority of the "native" electors seem to have been mulattoes, although a few Wolof names appear on the roll for Saint-Louis. During the nineteenth century the term habitant, and the superior status it implied, seem gradually to have become restricted to persons born locally of part-European ancestry.

In 1848, France briefly exchanged oligarchy for democratic republicanism. These new political principles, duly exported to Africa, created problems. The Second Republic reaffirmed that all French citizens were equal before the law: but at the same time, by abolishing colonial slavery and so extending the possibility of equal citizenship to large numbers of Africans not assimilated culturally, it made equality more difficult to implement. Senegal now became entitled to a representative in Paris; nearly five thousand electors were enrolled and in November 1848 over two thousand took part in an election which returned a mulatto, Durand-Valantin, to the National Assembly. But he resigned in 1850, unable to combine his representative functions with his business in Saint-Louis. At the by-election there were disputes over the distribution of voting cards and over the eligibility of the candidate returned, and no other Deputy was seated before the Second Empire temporarily terminated representative institutions in Senegal.[14]

[13] AAOF, 20 G 1 contains the electoral decree and lists of electors. The proceedings of the conseil-général are in 4 E 1.

[14] AAOF 20 G 3 gives electoral proceedings. I am indebted to M. Roger Pasquier for further information about Senegalese representation.

No Namierite has yet tried to disentangle the interplay of interests and personalities in these, the first elections in modern Africa. The careful racial balance in the *conseil-général*, the complaints made against the more democratic electorate of 1848, suggest that mulatto politicians were promoting causes and interests which differed from those favored by resident French merchants. Certainly the *habitant* community remained capable of taking independent stands, often on positions which showed traces of the radicalism of 1802. Later in the century, when the first unofficial Senegalese newspapers were promoted by independent mulatto traders, their editorial policies tended to be both anticlerical and anti-Muslim; favored the assimilation of colonial institutions to those of France; and, in opposition to the large French merchants, supported a speedy occupation of the Sudan.[15] Like their contemporaries the Sierra Leone Creoles, the Senegalese could thus combine radical political principles with strong support for the imperial expansion of their fatherland. But like them they were to find their remaining privileges threatened by the effects of the territorial expansion which they favored.

Dahomey

At the end of the eighteenth century the Aja states of the Slave Coast, and the Fon of Abomey in particular, seemed to be losing ground in the slave market. In the early decades of the nineteenth the trend was reversed; this region became the chief center of clandestine slaving north of the Equator, and the kingdom of Dahomey acquired international renown as a formidable military state, deplorably intractable in defense of its way of life. Three developments contributed to this change. One was the establishment of close family and commercial connections with one of the main transatlantic slave markets, Brazil. Portuguese subjects from Brazil, largely mulattoes of part-African descent, began to resettle on the Slave Coast in some numbers from the later eighteenth century, some in Whydah, some in Lagos, some in smaller independent states such as Porto Novo and the Popos. They brought Brazilian influences which have contributed to the culture of modern Dahomey—Catholic Christianity with strong syncretic traces of the American environment; patriarchal fam-

[15] Roger Pasquier, "Les Débuts de la presse au Sénégal," CEA, No. 7, p. 196.

ily patterns; distinctive styles of architecture, dance and cuisine.[16] They also brought commercial contacts notably with Bahia, which helped them to find export markets, not only for slaves but increasingly also for local produce and simple manufactures like cloth and hats.

Secondly, the Dahomean state profited from the gradual disintegration of the Yoruba empire of Oyo, its former overlord. This process began in the 1780s with the assertion of independence by the Bariba and Nupe peoples, but was greatly accelerated by the outbreak of a fierce civil war about 1821, and the almost simultaneous extension of the Fulani *jihad* into the northernmost Yoruba state of Ilorin. The effects on Dahomey of this period of confusion and interstate war among the Yoruba were to reduce the military pressure of a formerly powerful neighbor, thus enabling Abomey to denounce Oyo's suzerainty, and to provide a flow of marketable prisoners for the transatlantic trade, who were shipped through the ports of the western Slave Coast.

Thirdly, two able rulers, Gezo (1818-1858) and Gelele (1858-89), began to adapt the institutions of Dahomey to its changing international position. Gezo obtained the throne by a *coup d'état* in which he was assisted by a leading Portuguese Brazilian, F. F. da Souza. This man was rewarded by the hereditary title of *chacha* and the lucrative position of royal broker at Whydah; he and his countrymen continued to provide Gezo with commercial revenue and political advice. At first the revenue came almost completely from the reviving export of slaves, but this reflected sound appreciation of business opportunities rather than inherent inhumanity; after 1838 European merchants, notably the Marseille house of Régis, began to buy palm oil at the old French slaving fort of Whydah, and Brazilian and Dahomean middlemen quickly expanded their activities to utilize the new opportunities thus provided. Gezo supplemented the yield of forest trees by establishing royal plantations, tended by slaves withdrawn from the export market; taxation levied on private producers assisted the re-establishment of royal absolutism and provided the means to "bring back guns and powder to Dahomey." [17]

[16] Pierre Verger et al., Les Afro-Americains, Mémoires de l'IFAN, No. 27 (Dakar, 1953), p. 11 and passim.
[17] David A. Ross, "The Career of Domingo Martinez in the Bight of Benin, 1833-64," JAH VI, 80-81. See also Melville J. Herskovits, Dahomey: An Ancient West African Kingdom (New York, 1938), Vol. I, pp. 116, 128-31.

The economic revival of Dahomey, and the exports of slaves and oil on which it was successively based, aroused the interest of Europeans. The British government sporadically attempted to suppress the slave trade by negotiation or naval blockade; once it had taken control of Lagos in 1851 it became liable to entanglement in conflicts between Dahomey and its Yoruba neighbors. English Wesleyans and French and Portuguese Catholics established spiritual bridgeheads which Dahomean kings rightly feared might have political implications.[18] Régis, and later other French traders, were ready to invoke French political intervention in Dahomey and neighboring states like Porto Novo, not in order to set up formal colonial rule (which might not have suited them) but to ensure favorable conditions for their trade and to exclude British control.

Faced with a great intensification of such foreign activities at the very time when slave exports were ending in the 1860s, Gelele manoeuvred with much skill in defense of Dahomean independence. Old beliefs and practices were adapted to serve new needs. The tradition that kings of Dahomey must never look upon the sea provided a convenient justification for the court remaining at Abomey, ninety miles inland, beyond the range of naval artillery or landing parties; at Whydah relations with Europeans were conducted by the *Yavogan*, a royal functionary who employed the well known diplomatic expedient of referring inconvenient demands to his master. The essential purpose was to deter foreigners from mobilizing their strength against Dahomey; "he who makes the powder must win the battle," Gelele shrewdly commented.[19] European governments, particularly Britain with her repeatedly unhappy experiences in Ashanti, hesitated to launch military operations against formidable inland kingdoms; hence it suited Dahomey that her army and her king should have the reputation of formidable warriors—and notably cruel and barbaric ones at that. Even the practice of detaining European visitors to Abomey and compelling them to witness the annual human sacrifices to the national gods may have served a practical purpose, by discouraging visitors and enhancing the national reputation for "savagery." A few observers, like Sir Richard Burton, appreciated that nineteenth-century Dahomey was a declining power which might "crumble to pieces

[18] Paul Ellingworth, "Christianity and Politics in Dahomey, 1843-1867," *JAH*, V (1964), 209-220.
[19] Herskovits, *op. cit.*, I, 24.

with the first heavy shock";[20] but until the 1890s nobody administered the shock. Dahomey seemed to be succeeding better than most of the coastal states in absorbing commercial and cultural influences from Europe without radically transforming her traditional institutions and cosmology. How long this process could have continued without producing an internal crisis it is impossible to say, for it was ultimately to be cut short by French military action.

Ivory Coast

On the eastern Ivory Coast, a rather different pattern of relationships developed between French traders, the French government, and African authorities. The old pattern of off-shore trade, which still continued both west and east of Cape Palmas, was modified in 1843 by the establishment of fortified trading posts under the French flag at Assinie and Grand Bassam (and also in Gabon, where later a tiny settlement of freed slaves was established under the name of Libreville). These acts of state were motivated partly by apprehensions about British expansion, partly by pressure from Régis, the only French merchant interested in palm-oil trading. But neither Régis nor the representatives of the French state succeeded well in understanding or controlling the intricate mosaic of Ivoirian politics. At Grand Bassam, where it might have been possible to improve the position of the Nzima chief with whom they had signed a treaty, the French furthered the erosion of his authority; in the Ébrié lagoon they tried unsuccessfully to compel the cooperation of the "Jack-Jack" palm-oil brokers by establishing a third fort at Dabou in 1853; at Assinie the Agni kingdom of Kinjabo eventually provided access to some gold supplies, but resisted all attempts to by-pass its territory and open more direct trade with interior markets. The French hoped to find *protégés* who would protect their trade as effectively as the king of Dahomey, but they were not prepared themselves to make serious efforts to provide the political and economic advantages which such African associates might expect in return. All parties thus became disillusioned. By 1857 Régis, having failed to manipulate French power with sufficient success, withdrew to seek more profitable trade on noncolonial coasts; French garrisons were left to protect a series of ephemeral and undercapitalized trading ventures until the Franco-Prussian war provided an opportunity for military withdrawal.

[20] Richard F. Burton, *A Mission to Gelele, King of Dahomey* (Memorial edition, London, 1893), Vol. II, pp. 57, 87, 155-6; cf. P. Bouche, *La Côte des Esclaves et le Dahomey* (Paris, 1885), pp. 398-400.

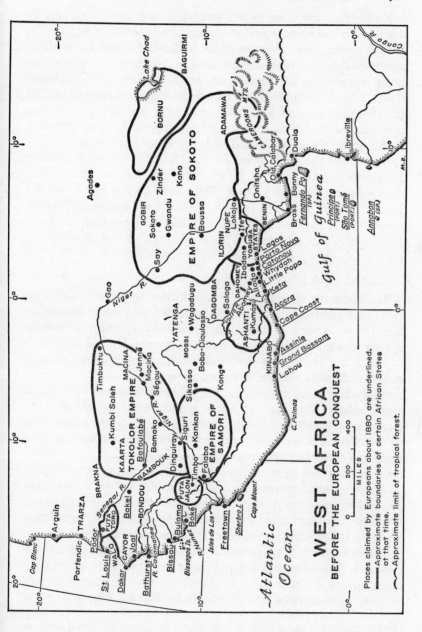

WEST AFRICA

BEFORE THE EUROPEAN CONQUEST

Places claimed by Europeans about 1880 are underlined.

—— Approximate boundaries of certain African States at that time.

〰️ Approximate limit of tropical forest.

For the next few years, French sovereignty was represented only by a flag which had been somewhat apprehensively entrusted to a Dutch-backed trading house, Verdier of La Rochelle. Ultimately, Verdier's agents made considerable contributions to Ivoirian economic development, founding coffee plantations, prospecting for gold, exploring routes toward the Sudan and finally disproving the legend of the impassable mountains of Kong. But until 1878 Verdier's concern was rather to use the authority of the French state to build up a trading monopoly at the coast (shared with the English house of Swanzy) and to crush the competition of the "Esquires," English-speaking traders from other parts of Africa. French power was present only nominally until the later 1880s. The effects on the peoples of the Ivory Coast of the "fifty years of political and commercial hesitations" [21] after 1843 were not profound; they were confined to coastal peoples who jealously guarded their privileges as brokers or agents for a slowly changing and expanding foreign trade.

Faidherbe and Inland Penetration

To Europeans anxious to regenerate Africa by promoting civilization and commerce, all these coastal activities were rather disappointing. By midcentury a reaction was evident, especially in Britain, against high-minded attempts forcibly to prevent Africans from dealing in slaves, and against the missionaries and philanthropists associated with such policies. Whereas some critics concluded that it would be best for all concerned if foreigners would simply leave Africa alone, others believed that better results might be obtained by European penetration of the interior. Since the great journeys of Mungo Park explorers had successively revealed the existence of large organized states in the Western Sudan which might provide better customers and collaborators than the petty principalities of the coast. These conclusions, empirically arrived at in the first place, were now fortified by two general propositions which secured wide acceptance. One was that Islam could provide a moralizing and stabilizing force, which even Christians might recognize as more suitable for contemporary African needs than European Christianity with its cultural appendages. The other idea, derived partly from prejudice, partly from contemporary scientific misconceptions, was that Africans in interior districts were somehow "purer" than those deemed to have been cor-

[21] Subtitle of the useful work of Paul Atger, *La France en Côte-d'Ivoire de 1843 à 1893* (Dakar, 1962).

rupted (whether genetically or culturally) by contact with European slave-dealers or missionaries.

These were primarily British ideas. Until the 1860s the major exploring journeys to the western Sudan were made either by British travellers or by Germans in British service. Apart from René Caillié's remarkable pilgrimage from the River Nunez to Timbuktu, French activities south of the desert were confined to reconnaissances of the Senegambian hinterland and Futa Jalon. Moreover, admiration for the organizing capacity of Islam was often tempered by hostility, especially in those who had personal experience of Arab resistance to France in Algeria. Many Frenchmen believed that if the interior was worth reaching at all it would have to be reached by armed force, against implacable Muslim resistance. But Algeria did not affect all Frenchmen like this; even military officers might be influenced by an alternative French tradition, of scholarly interest and respect for Islamic culture. Such a man, Captain Louis Faidherbe, governed Senegal from 1854 until 1861, and again in 1863-65.

Although many Frenchmen have written brief eulogies of Faidherbe's work in Senegal nobody has yet attempted a major biographical study, and conflicting interpretations are still possible of this energetic and imperious proconsul. The conditions of his appointment enabled him to write a large signature upon French African policy; holding office over an extended period in a colony noted for ephemeral governorships, he often succeeded in imposing his views on the ministers of the Second Empire, a regime which welcomed successes abroad but lacked any clear doctrine or program for securing them. Faidherbe was inspired by a vision of French influence extending into the supposedly rich lands of the middle Niger. This vision was in many respects illusory, and Faidherbe himself could move only slowly and erratically towards it; but its siren attractions were to exercise a decisive influence on the development of French policy under his successors.

At the time of Faidherbe's appointment Al Hajj 'Umar was threatening to invade Futa Toro and the danger of a general *jihad* was alarming the colonial community. This peril had to be taken seriously and much of Faidherbe's early activity was therefore concentrated on military action to consolidate France's position against Muslim states of the lower Senegal valley. He established a new fort at Medina in 1855 and its heroic defence by Paul Holle two years later diverted 'Umar from the Senegal to the Niger valley; this success was hailed in Saint-Louis as a turning point in Senegalese history. Meanwhile Faidherbe established more direct control over Walo; defeated the Trarzas and commuted their "tribute" on the gum trade to a fixed export duty of 3%; extended French influence in the Sine, Saloum, and Casamance valleys; and intervened (more actively than successfully) in the internal politics of Futa Toro and Cayor.

Although these operations put French power in Senegal on a far stronger basis than ever before, they did not everywhere establish direct French control. Cayor provides a good example of the experimental approach of Faidherbe and his successors to collaboration with African rulers. The export trade in groundnuts, which was at last expanding the colonial economy, gave this state a crucial importance, both as a producing area and as controlling overland communications between Saint-Louis and the new commercial ports of Rufisque and Dakar (occupied by the French in 1857). Faidherbe tried to install a subservient *damel*, Madiodio; but he chose his man badly. It was Lat-Dior who, by assuming the leadership of Islamic revival, secured the support of the country. Faidherbe's successors, hoping that the spread of Islam would restrain the brigands known as *tiédos* and lead to increased production of groundnuts, came to see Lat-Dior as a ruler with whom cooperation might be possible and fruitful. But after 1877 French plans to build a railway through Cayor led to demands which Lat-Dior could not accept; knowing that this "steamship on dry land" would eventually erode Cayor's independence he withheld collaboration, and eventually died resisting the French in 1886.[22]

Faidherbe's intensive military activity did not preclude policies of improvement within the colony. Nor did this mean merely administrative reorganization and public works. He was the first governor to understand that France's future in Senegal depended on her success in permitting Africans to become her loyal subjects while remaining good Muslims. He therefore recognized and regulated the position of Islamic courts within colonial territory, founded a school to train youths from the interior as interpreters and emissaries of French influence, initiated serious attempts to study and understand African societies. He raised a battalion of *tirailleurs sénégalais*, devising conditions of service which for the first time permitted the recruitment of a stable and efficient African army.

These internal reforms provided a firm base for Faidherbe's wider

[22] Vincent Monteil, "Lat-Dior et l'Islamisation des Wolofs," *Archives de Sociologie des Religions*, XVI (1963).

imperial strategy. To the north, after his settlement with the Trarzas, he sent expeditions into the Mauritanian desert—seeing it not merely as the source of the now declining gum trade, but as a route toward France's other growing empire in North Africa. In 1860-61 Bou-el-Moghdad, a Senegalese Muslim in French service, travelled overland to Mogador and Algiers, proclaiming France's benevolence toward Islam in the hope of offsetting the growing prestige of Al Hajj 'Umar among the desert people.[23] In the south Faidherbe aimed to extend French influence as far as Futa Jalon, and to establish a fort in the Nunez estuary. To facilitate commercial and military control of the region he urged Louis Napoleon's government to negotiate the withdrawal of Portugal and Britain from their respective enclaves on the coast; to secure British Gambia Faidherbe was willing to surrender the *comptoirs* on the Ivory Coast and at Gabon, for which he foresaw little future. He thus launched the idea of a territorial exchange which now became a recurrent theme of inter-European relations in West Africa.

By consolidating a French empire in Senegambia Faidherbe hoped to form a secure base for inland penetration toward the Niger. But, unlike successors who invoked his name to justify their military campaigns, Faidherbe hoped to achieve this penetration by negotiation backed only indirectly by force. Just as contemporaries in Britain looked for "strong native governments" capable of protecting the activities of traders and missionaries, so Faidherbe made some efforts to associate African states with his purposes. (Comparable experiments had been tried even in Algeria, in short-lived attempts to work with the great Arab chief Abd-el-Kadr).[24] In the Sudan, Al Hajj 'Umar provided the test case; by 1857 it seemed that neither the Tokolors nor the French could destroy the other's power in the immediate future, and so there might be mutual advantages in collaboration. In 1860 Faidherbe negotiated a demarcation line along the Bafing river with a Tokolor emissary, and provisionally agreed to send his own ambassador to discuss future relations with 'Umar. His hope

---

[23] *AAOF*—1 G. 27. Bou-el-Moghdad to Flize, Nov. 24, 1860, Bou-el-Moghdad, "Voyage par Terre entre le Sénégal et le Maroc," *Revue Maritime et Coloniale*, I (1861).

[24] When these attempts failed, the French successfully sought to work with religious leaders of the Tijaniyya: Jamil M. Abun-Nasr, *The Tijaniyya*, Chapter IV. For French relations with Al Hajj 'Umar see Chapter V of this work; also John D. Hargreaves, "The Tokolor Empire of Ségou and Its Relations with the French," *Boston University Papers on Africa*, II (Boston, 1966).

was that, in return for political support and supplies of firearms, the Tokolors would permit France to construct a line of fortified trading posts from Senegal to a base for navigation on the Niger. With their cooperation, Faidherbe hoped to push French trade and influence downstream and avert the monopoly which Britain, through her traders in the delta, threatened to establish over this great waterway.

But this ambassador, Lieutenant Mage, set out only in October 1863, by which time rebellions against the Tokolor state had begun, and such collaboration seemed a less attractive policy. Mage was detained over two years in Ségou, and when he got back to Saint-Louis Faidherbe had retired. His successor Laprade (formerly in charge of Gorée and Dakar) was preoccupied with the southern rivers of Guinea (where he founded the fort which Faidherbe had proposed for the Nunez, together with others in the Pongos and the Mellacourie.) Mage's report did not encourage him to turn toward the Sudan. In Paris, Louis Napoleon and his ministers were equally unenthusiastic. West Africa was an unpromising field for winning Imperial laurels; the costs of an active policy seemed certain to outweigh any satisfactions which might be gained.

So Faidherbe's imperial schemes were filed away. In 1869, Governor Valière was instructed to avoid new annexations and pursue the policy of peaceful consolidation favored by merchants in Bordeaux; within two weeks of his arrival he was advocating a withdrawal of attempts at direct control from Cayor, the annexed provinces of Futa Toro, even from Walo, and a return to less direct methods of exercising influence.[25] The trauma of the Franco-Prussian war merely reinforced reactions against active West African policies, which operated in France on much the same lines as in contemporary Britain. In Cayor Valière restored Lat-Dior, whom Faidherbe had deposed; in Futa Toro and other parts of the lower Senegal valley he sought to cooperate with independent chiefs who enjoyed the support of their subjects; he abandoned all immediate thought of penetrating the Tokolor Empire. During the 1870s, French influence was still felt more or less indirectly, even in the Senegal valley; it represented potentially the strongest force in the local balance of power, but there still remained ample scope for independent African initiative. The scramble for direct European control had not yet begun.

[25] ANSOM, Sénégal I/56/a Rigault de Genouilly to Valière, Sep. 25t 1869; Sénégal I/56/b Valière to M.M.C. 364, Oct. 31, 1869; 142, April 14, 1870.

SEVEN

The French Conquest

The significance and origins of the "new Imperialism" which transformed the map of Africa during the last three decades of the nineteenth century have been incessantly discussed, in contexts extending far beyond the limits of French expansion in West Africa. The key to the violent new departures which transformed the nature of Afro-European relations must be sought primarily in Europe, for it was from European governments that the great innovations came. Some hypotheses seek to explain imperialism by reference to new needs resulting from profound changes in the economic structures and drives of European countries, or to changing relationships on European society. More empirically-minded historians concentrate on the background to what have been called "microevents": the personalities of the imperialists and the manifold pressures (economic, political, ideological, and bureaucratic) which influenced their day-to-day decisions. These two approaches are not incompatible, for microevents need to be related to profound changes as well as to accidental contingencies. But clearly it is primarily the detailed empirical study that is needed to discover what characteristics distinguish French expansion in West Africa from other manifestations of the "new imperialism." Briefly, it seems to have owed less to pressure from persons interested in the economic resources of the area than to initiatives of local military commanders or governors, taking advantage of opportunities for glory provided by changing political conditions in France. Expansion carried out in this way tended to level out African authorities which failed to comply with the simple imperatives of military expediency, and so cause some rather sharp breaks in the continuity of African history.

97

The Thrust to the Sudan

In 1876 the pacific Valière was succeeded as Governor of Senegal by Colonel Brière de l'Isle of the French Marine Infantry: an active, forceful man with ambitions to execute Faidherbe's testament in the Southern Rivers and the Sudan. But whereas Faidherbe hoped to protect traders travelling from the Senegal to the Niger by armed diplomacy and forts, Brière in 1878 added ambitious plans to build a railway, prepared after Paul Soleillet, explorer and railway enthusiast, had passed through Saint-Louis on his way to Ségou.[1] Although the Niger line, even on the original optimistic costing, was not one from which any company or individual (except perhaps contractors) could calculate to profit, French Ministers persuaded Parliament to vote funds with which to begin a truncated compromise project; they thus committed themselves to the first stage of a long, costly, and embarrassing program, which eventually took a quarter of a century to get its first train from the head of navigation on the Senegal to the Niger.

Brière's schemes implied political control. In 1880 Captain J. S. Gallieni, having explored the political situation in the upper Senegal basin, left with an armed party on a new mission to Amadu, son and successor of Al Hajj 'Umar. At first Gallieni's idea was to win the friendship of Amadu's Mandinka and Bambara subjects, and so prepare the break-up of the Tokolor state and the establishment of direct French influence in its place; but after reaching Bamako with a depleted party he discovered that Amadu's authority was still well founded on the right bank of the Niger. To exclude British influence he negotiated a Treaty, which he believed to establish a French protectorate; and for a time Gallieni took seriously the possibility of tactical collaboration with the Tokolors. But meanwhile, to cover the railway-building operations, a strong French column under Colonel Desbordes had entered Amadu's provinces in the Senegal valley. Most of its officers were hostile to Islam in principle, and anxious for military glory; Desbordes was contemptuous of Gallieni's intellectual volatility, and prepared to coexist with Muslim states only temporarily, on the basis of purest expediency. Henceforth schemes for collaborating with African kings tended to be trumped by the

[1] ANSOM Sénégal, I/61/c Brière, 350, April 21, 1878.

ace of military necessity. Garbled versions of the exploits of the African columns could win patriotic cheers from Frenchmen who had little knowledge of, or concrete interest in, West Africa. Although politicians from time to time applied restraints, out of prudence or economy, the Republic was now effectively committed to advance on an African frontier whose moving force was represented by ambitious military officers of middle rank.

In two other sections of western Africa, the French government gave some support to forward elements during the early 1880s. In the lower Congo region an Italian-born officer of the French navy, Savorgnan de Brazza, had been exploring routes toward that great waterway at Stanley Pool; in October 1882 the government decided to ratify his treaty with the Batéké, and discreetly to support his further activities on this new frontier. Brazza, an attractive and courageous personality, had become a popular figure with the French public and press; in supporting him the French government provided some vicarious compensation to nationalists who felt that France had been cheated and outmanoeuvred by the British occupation of Egypt. It was a policy, writes a Belgian scholar, "dictated much more by patriotic enthusiasm than by material considerations." [2] In January 1883 Jauréguibery, a former Governor of Senegal become Minister of Marine, authorized the re-establishment of the French protectorate at Porto Novo, and also in the small Popos trading states, despatched a French warship to visit Bonny, Brass, and Calabar in the Niger delta; and proposed to try and develop a special position in the Benué valley. The direct and immediate consequences of these initiatives, which seemed to threaten French control in areas where British trade was important, included British countermeasures to reserve the future of the lower Niger, an unexpected intervention by Germany in Togo and Cameroon, and a sudden scramble by European powers to appropriate stretches of African coastline and exclude the danger of foreign tariffs.

It looked as though Europe had embarked on a full-scale invasion of Africa; but in the short run this impression was slightly misleading. European governments were still anxious to limit their financial and political liabilities; their Foreign Ministries in particular hesitated to

[2] Jean Stengers, "L'Impérialisme colonial de la fin du xixᵉ siècle: mythe ou réalité." *JAH*, III (1962), 477.

become committed to new quarrels with their neighbors simply for the sake of African territories of speculative economic value. Once the British National African Company succeeded in buying out French trading interests from the lower Niger, Premier Jules Ferry assented to France's exclusion from that crucial region, subject to rather weak international safeguards negotiated at the Berlin Conference of 1884-85. The rather fierce intercolonial disputes which had developed along the coasts were all eventually adjusted by bilateral boundary agreements negotiated in Europe. The chauvinistic interest in colonial territory which had suddenly appeared in France (as elsewhere) in the years 1882-85, was temporarily dampened by a minor military defeat in Indo-China in 1885; disenchantment prevailed among Parliamentarians. Work on the Niger railway, now recognizably a white elephant, was curtailed, and by 1890 had reached only Bafoulabé; the military forces of Haut-Sénégal-Niger, hindered by physical difficulties and by Muslim revolts in their rear, were held on the leash; in Dahomey France remained reluctant to resolve her difficulties by a major military expedition. Only after 1890 did serious drives to occupy the interior begin. Within ten years they had established French control over an extent of country impressively large on the map, but not apparently very rich or (the Mossi states excepted) very populous.

During the 1890s pressure groups developed in France, concerned to influence African policy and disseminate information about it. Their chief spokesman was Eugène Etienne, an Algerian-born deputy who as under-Secretary for Colonies in 1887 and 1889-92 increased the importance of his office in the direction of full Ministerial status. Etienne dreamed of extending French influence toward Lake Chad from Senegal, Congo, and Mediterranean; in 1890 he encouraged the formation of the *Comité d'Afrique française*, a body which sponsored its own armed expeditions in attempts to increase the French stake in the partition of Africa. In 1892 Etienne became chairman of a group of 91 colonially-minded deputies drawn from all parts of the Chamber; next year bankers and merchants with colonial interests came together in the *Union Coloniale française*. But the seeds of the future French colonies already existed in West Africa before the emergence of organized imperialism in France; one judgment is that the new movements merely "rationalized the blunders and paper claims of the nineties and persuaded the French people to do their duty and turn them into good colonies." [3]

Even in 1890, there were yet plenty of blunders to be made. The timing and methods of the French advances in the Sudan were often determined by the somewhat wayward decisions of the military governors on the spot—notably by the ruthless and ambitious Colonel Archinard.[4] His actions frequently distressed the imperialist movement and the civilians in the colonial ministry; but with some setbacks the military retained a high degree of initiative until 1899, thanks to Brière, Desbordes, and other former comrades holding important bureaucratic appointments in Paris. As far as other European powers were concerned the partition was completed peacefully, though not uneventfully. The Lake Chad area, which from 1890 became the target of French penetration from north, south, and west, was not of such intrinsic importance as would justify European powers in moving near the brink of war. In 1897-98 relations with Britain became tense when the French tried to occupy land on the lower Niger, and so reopen the question of international control; but both countries felt they had more at stake in the Nile than in the Niger, and it was Fashoda that saw the major Anglo-French confrontation in Africa. Temporarily the ardor of French colonial expansionists greatly exacerbated relations with Britain; yet in the end Europeans succeeded in dividing up Africa without any major conflict among themselves.

Samori and the French Military

African states were profoundly affected by the leading role of the military in advancing the French frontier. British colonies which expanded on the initiatives of trading companies or administrations open to mercantile pressure were more likely to try to expand their influence peacefully, or to preserve the institutions of conquered customers, than the forceful Marine officers of French Sudan. The Tokolor state was the first target of their military ambitions. In February 1889 Archinard suddenly attacked their fortress at Koundian;

[3] JAH, II (1961), 160: Ronald Robinson's review of the important work of Henri Brunschwig, Mythes et Réalités de l'Impérialisme colonial français (Paris, 1960).

[4] Important new light is thrown on the French imperialist movement by the thesis of Mr. A. S. Kanya-Forstner, "The French in West Africa: a Study in Military Imperialism" (Ph.D. thesis, Cambridge, 1965).

when this exploit failed to win the promotion he coveted, he proceeded to occupy Ségou (from which Amadu, however, had already prudently removed his capital). These unauthorized actions committed France to the forcible destruction of the Tokolor state. Militarily this was not too difficult, apart from a humiliating defeat by Tuareg near Timbuktu in January 1894; the Tokolors withdrew, resisting, into the empire of Sokoto. But these campaigns destroyed any lingering possibility that a French West African Empire might somehow accommodate itself to the survival of a powerful Muslim state.

Farther south, this lesson was also learned by a new Mandinka empire which had confronted the French since 1882. This state is usually distinguished from its Fula predecessors as owing less to the sanctity and learning of its founder, more to his organizing ability and the fierce military prowess of his soldiers. Alimani Samori was no Koranic scholar and certainly no mystic; but this is not to say that he can be dismissed as a "nominal Muslim," a mere "adventurer." The Touré clan to which he belonged were Muslim *dyulas*, widely dispersed through the Western Sudan, but his immediate ancestors, settled in the Milo valley for over a century, had taken to cattle-herding, intermarried with the animist Kamaras, reverted to ancestor-worship, and gradually loosened their ties with the Muslim community. Samori's reconversion began during his travels as a young *dyula*, probably in the years 1846-51, and these journeys must have taken him to places strongly influenced by Al Hajj 'Umar; but it was not until about 1880, when military success had already made him master of a sizeable empire, that he gave much emphasis to the idea of *jihad* to convert the heathen. He was a limping pupil of the mallams, and his state left no contribution to the literature of African Islam. But mosques were built in the lands he conquered, ritual prayer and other Koranic practices enforced, *marabouts* held in esteem; Samori may not have satisfied the orthodox but he was more than a nominal Muslim; even his critics admit that his conquests "prepared the way for a more positive acceptance" [5] of Islam among the Mandinka, and other subjects of his empire.

There is some ambiguity in modern African attitudes to Samori.

[5] J. Spencer Trimingham, A *History of Islam in West Africa* (London, 1962), p, 162. Samori's career is being studied by M. Yves Person, and much of this paragraph is based upon his two remarkable articles, "Les Ancêtres de Samori," *CEA*, No. 13, pp. 125-51: "La jeunesse de Samori," *Revue française d'histoire d'Outre-Mer* (1962), pp. 151-80.

Although there is evidence that, like other Muslim state-builders, he appealed to the more mobile elements in Sudanic societies (traders, *griots*, men who had visited the European settlements) against the chiefs and their associates, his was in no real sense a modernizing state. The administrative structure described by Péroz in 1887, with 162 former chiefdoms organized in ten provinces and providing revenue in the form of gold and agricultural produce, did not have time to mature and develop; Samori's provincial governors were too often engaged in fighting, and by methods which brought great suffering to their African opponents. Villages were destroyed, men and women were put cruelly to death or sold as slaves so that the proceeds might purchase European arms from around Sierra Leone, and cavalry mounts from Ségou, Mossi, and Macina. Guns and cartridges were also made by Samori's African blacksmiths.[6] In some parts of Guinea, Samori's descendant Sekou Touré, when seeking support for his nationalist party had to face the apprehensive query "You will not sell us into slavery?"[7] And yet there is little doubt that Sekou Touré's ancestry has been more of an asset than a liability in his political career. Among modern nationalists seeking to reassert the African identity, Samori has earned increasing posthumous esteem from his courageous and often skillful defense of his independence.

Samori's first clash with the French occurred in February 1882, soon after Colonel Desbordes' military column had reached the Niger. But for the next nine years French attitudes remained ambiguous. The military knew that their lines of communication were still precarious; and political and administrative authorities in France were anxious to avoid major military commitments in Africa, although they were not always able to control their commanders on the spot. They therefore temporized, exploiting the divisions which existed among their African neighbors. After the failure of a premature attempt by Colonel Combes to drive Samori out of the gold-bearing province of Bouré, the French made two treaties with Samori; the second, negotiated by Péroz in February 1887, imposed a frontier along the Niger and Tankisso rivers and (according to the French text) established a French protectorate over Samori's empire. The

[6] Etienne Péroz, *Au Soudan Français*, Chapter IX (Paris, 1889). See also Martin Legassick, "Firearms, Horses and Samorian Army Organization, 1870-1898," *JAH*, VII (1966), 95-115.

[7] Ruth Schachter Morgenthau, *Political Parties in French-Speaking West Africa* (Oxford, 1964), pp. 234-5.

French military never intended this treaty to last; they encouraged trouble between Samori and Amadu, and supplied arms for use against their protégé to Tiéba, a Muslim Senufo who was building up a formidable state of his own at Sikasso.

Understanding something at least of French duplicity, Samori sought support from Britain. Shortly after Combes' attack of 1885, Samori sent messengers to Sierra Leone (with which he had first made contact in 1879-80), seeking to encourage trade and secure political support. Among Freetown Africans and British traders some feeling developed in favor of an alliance with Samori, who they hoped might hold back the French advance and so open that road to the Western Sudan of which many Sierra Leoneans dreamed. They welcomed the prospect of trade with Samori and began to sell him, not merely the unreliable flintlocks used in earlier African wars, but modern precision weapons. The British government, however, would not commit themselves to support Samori, or any other African ruler, at risk of war with France. British officials encouraged trade and good relations with Samori (to the distress of the Africans he threatened, who looked to Freetown for protection); but London ignored his offer to come under British protection, and in the Brussels Treaty of 1890 agreed to restrict the sale of precision arms in Africa. Anglo-French relations might be strained, but in dealing with a strong African state the needs of European solidarity asserted themselves.

By the beginning of 1891, after Amadu had been driven from Ségou, Samori realized his peril and tardily sought an understanding with the Tokolors. It was too late. In April Archinard launched an attack toward Kankan, intending to separate Samori from Sierra Leone. Outright war now began; to the French surprise it lasted, intermittently, for seven years, thanks to the courage of Samori's troops, their foreign arms, and the skill of their commander. Whereas the Tokolors built fortresses, which could not withstand the arrival of French artillery, Samori fought an open campaign, retiring eastward and actually transferring the machinery of their state toward the northern Ivory Coast and the Upper Volta, scorching the earth at the expense of its inhabitants. Once in the neighborhood of Kong he tried unsuccessfully to re-establish relations with the British on the Gold Coast, rejecting overtures to collaborate with King Prempeh of Ashanti. But there was still little chance of British support against France, although when Anglo-French relations were tense in 1898,

Joseph Chamberlain seemed to contemplate some "arrangement." [8] In 1898, inevitably, Samori was captured; he died in exile two years later.

Military Rule and African Authority

Clearly there was never much hope of collaboration between partners so imperious as Samori and Archinard. But even when faced by less formidable opponents, French commanders rarely made much attempt to comprehend or tolerate; chiefs of the countries they controlled, especially if they were Muslims suspected of having contacts with the enemies of France, were liable to be deposed on calculations of immediate expediency. Sometimes they were arbitrarily replaced by French nominees without a vestige of claim in traditional law. A former employee of the Senegalese telegraph service, Mademba, was appointed ruler of the important town of Sansanding on the Niger;[9] after the conquest of Macina Amadu's half-brother Aguibou was ensconced for a few years, cross-posted from Dinguiray like a French prefect.

These were perhaps extreme cases. Often the conditions of their conquest obliged the French to make rudimentary experiments with the institutions, and even with the theory, of what the British were to call Indirect Rule. Archinard, knowing that he would never have the resources to provide all the villages of the Sudan with the French administrators whom he believed they would welcome, urged his *commandants de cercle* to study African institutions and to leave the administration of local affairs in the hands of local rulers, ideally "men who are devoted to us but who, by reason of their family and their origin, can be accepted by the natives as natural chiefs, not as imposed rulers." [10] These admirable principles were not easy to execute. After occupying Ségou, for example, Archinard tentatively installed as *fama* Mari-Diara, heir to the Bambara dynasty overthrown by Al Hajj 'Umar and defined restricted functions for him to dis-

---

[8] *Documents Diplomatiques Français*, 1st series, XII, No. 156, Howard to Hanotaux, Sept. 26, 1895. G. E. Metcalfe, *Documents of Ghana History* (Accra, 1964), pp. 496-8; Chamberlain to Maxwell, Conf. June 4, 1897. See also William Tordoff, *Ashanti under the Prempehs* (London, 1965), pp. 64-6, 90.

[9] On him see Abd-el-Kader Mademba, "Au Sénégal et au Soudan français," *BCEHSAOF*, XIII (1930).

[10] Archinard's report on the campaign of 1890-91, partially reproduced in Jacques Méniaud, *Les Pionniers du Soudan* (Paris, 1931), II, 54-6.

charge under the supervision of the French Resident.[11] But Mari-Diara's view of the powers appropriate to a *fama* of Ségou exceeded these peremptorily imposed limits; within weeks he and other notables were summarily executed for conspiracy, and the French turned to seek more pliable subordinates in the rival Massassi dynasty. But the Massassis, former rulers of Kaarta, aroused fierce resistance when imposed on the Bambaras of Ségou; nor can their authority have been strengthened by the nightly humiliations which the Commandant used to impose upon their subjects in order to gratify the warped sense of humor of the officers' mess.[12] From the very start the reality of French control was apparent beneath the withering superstructure of African institutions.

It was military officers, largely inspired with the same ideas and values as Archinard, who first established French rule throughout the great Sudanic empire conquered from the base at Kayes—a vast territory including not only modern Mali, but Upper Volta, Niger, and substantial parts of Guinea and the Ivory Coast. Although Sudan received its first civilian Governor, a controversial political appointment, in 1893, civilian control was not effectively established until the twentieth century. In Niger, among the martial Berber tribes of the desert marches, and also in the other military empire of Mauritania,[13] military government continued into the 1920s, and military influence remained strong after that. Ironically, these officers, many of whom fiercely rejected the revolutionary tradition in France, carried through a levelling of traditional distinctions in Sudanic society comparable

[11] Speech by Archinard, April 11, 1890, Méniaud, *op. cit.*, I, 517-20.
[12] P. L. Monteil, *De Saint Louis à Tripoli* (Paris, 1895), p. 23. On Bambara resistance, see Louis Tauxier, *Histoire des Bambaras* (Paris, 1942), pp. 182-206.
[13] This could well form a separate chapter. Faidherbe's reconnaissances into Mauritania (p. 95 above) were not followed by major French attempts at penetration until the twentieth century. The Trans-Saharan railway scheme was set back by the destruction of Colonel Flatters' mission to the Hoggar in 1881, and those responsible for colonial policy were reluctant to increase their military commitments. Only after 1901, when the Sudan was largely occupied and French policy began to press more heavily upon Morocco, did it seem urgent to increase French influence in Mauritania. From 1901 until his violent death in 1905 Coppolani, an Islamic specialist, resumed an active policy of "peaceful penetration"; thereafter, as the connection between Mauritanian and Moroccan affairs became more apparent, France used military force to establish her control, drastically depleting the country's livestock in the process. Resistance was strong until 1920, and frequent "police operations" continued into the 1930s. See Geneviève Désiré-Vuillemin, *Contribution à l'histoire de la Mauritanie* (Dakar, 1962).

only to the work of the great Revolution of 1789. They did not every-where need to act quite so drastically as in the vacuums left by their defeat of Amadu and Samori. In Mossi, notably, although the oc-cupying forces overthrew a Mogho Naba who had defended his country's independence (first by diplomacy, ultimately by arms) they did not follow through their original intention of encouraging the fragmentation of the country. It proved more expedient to seek the collaboration, in the unpopular tasks of recruiting labor and collecting taxes, of men who would be acknowledged as legitimate heirs of the Mogho Nabas. Hence, while France maintained strict control over all matters with political implications, later Nabas who would ac-cept such a role were permitted to retain or recover certain ceremonial, judicial, and minor administrative functions, and ultimately to resume political influence also.[14] But in general, the Napoleonic approach of the conquerors led them to overthrow African state structures and establish military-type hierarchies under French authority.

Occupation of the Coastal Colonies

In the coastal districts, civilians played a larger role in the ex-tension of French power; and they usually tried, though with varying success, to cooperate with established traders who might be anxious to maintain the basic structure of those states with whom they did business. During the 1880s and 1890s the primary French concern was to obtain treaties of protection which would exclude other Euro-pean powers; in principle they had no objection to leaving African rulers to exercise functions of internal sovereignty. In practice, their systems of indirect control proved unworkable. In the southern Ivory Coast, writes Atger, they

did not permit the constitution of genuine autonomous African states, nor even the maintenance of the chiefdoms already existing. Local commandants were neither to forbid wars and palavers, nor to become involved in them. They found themselves obliged to intervene, willy-nilly; they then put their available forces at the service of the traders, not of their African allies. The former could count on the support of the local comandants to ensure the maintenance of their freedom to trade, where that was menaced; the latter received no help in strengthen-

[14] Elliott P. Skinner, *The Mossi of the Upper Volta* (Stanford, 1964), Chapters IX & X.

ing their authority over their subject, or those whom they claimed as their subjects. Far from fortifying their position or contributing to the modernization of their states, the French protectorate finally destroyed their power.[15]

Eventually, with or without the use of military force, the French tightened their control. Although in places it was exercised in forms which preserved rather more of the former political structure than in conquered territories, its ultimate effects were hardly less far-reaching.

In the rivers of Guinea the military outposts established by Laprade languished for a dozen years without exercising any decisive influence on the complexities of local politics, until Brière launched a more active policy to exclude the British influence still represented by traders and government agents from Sierra Leone. Diplomacy secured a renunciation of British rights in 1882, but France's position among the coastal peoples remained precarious; fierce and sometimes indiscriminate military intervention was needed before French control was complete in these rivers, where old political disputes could still be exacerbated by European intervention. By the time French "pacification" was complete few rulers in the coastal area seem to have retained much authority beyond that which derived from the power of their new protectors. In Futa Jalon it proved expedient to maintain some form of collaboration with the Alimamies a little longer; the first protectorate treaty was simply a diplomatic instrument to bar British claims, and only after 25 years of increasingly direct control did the French deliberately begin to break up this historic Muslim state and administer its separate provinces through petty canton chiefs. Eventually even less survived of traditional African structures in Guinea than in other colonies.[16]

Dahomey, strongest of the coastal kingdoms, began to experience increasing foreign pressure during the 1880s. European intervention seemed to become more, not less, likely as Dahomey abandoned the slaving activities that had made her notorious. Britain's occupation of Lagos in 1861 alarmed the few Marseillais traders on the Slave Coast,

[15] Atger, La France en Côte-d'Ivoire (Dakar, 1962), p. 184.
[16] J. Suret-Canale, "La Guinée dans le système colonial," Présence Africaine, XXIX (1959-60), 13-8.

who feared they might be denied access to their palm-oil supplies except through British customhouses; they therefore sought to commit their government to the protecting of the principality of Porto Novo. It was not easy to find collaborators on the African side; but after 1874 Tofa, an ambitious young ruler of Porto Novo, proved willing to accept French support maintaining dynastic claims against internal rivals, and upholding Porto Novan independence against Gelele, his nominal overlord. By 1883 the French government had been led, by pressure from interested parties and by accidents of international politics, to proclaim a protectorate at Porto Novo and occupy the neighboring Dahomean port of Cotonou. They also planned to protect the four small Popos states to the westward; but German commercial and missionary influence had been growing here and in 1884-85, through developments which had more to do with European than with African politics, Little Popo and Porto Seguro were incorporated in the German protectorate of Togoland. Portugal too, alarmed by the signs of the coming scramble, sent a few troops in 1885 to reaffirm her sovereignty over her old fort at Whydah, which technically remained part of Portugal until 1961.

In Abomey the ageing Gelele saw his former power and independence gravely threatened. French soldiers occupied what had become his busiest port, and protected Tofa, whom he considered a revolted vassal; French missionaries were beginning to undermine the inherited beliefs of his subjects. But the French, still influenced by the myths of Dahomean power, hesitated to add to their military commitments in Africa, and Gelele was either too prudent or too feeble to provoke them. In 1889 however he was succeeded by Behanzin, a man determined to assert Dahomey's independence, to resist French attempts to consolidate and formalize their control of Cotonou, and to strike down the pretensions of Tofa. Although the French moved prudently, conscious of military weakness and domestic diversions, by 1892 they could no longer tolerate Behanzin's militant independence, and their troops occupied Abomey. The commander, General Dodds, who was of Senegalese birth and descent and had some feeling for African politics, tried to find a means of governing through Behanzin before deposing him in January 1894; but thereafter the kingdom was divided into its eighteenth-century nuclei, Abomey and Allada, and for a few years France tried to rule indirectly through the royal lineages.[17] In Porto Novo, Tofa, for services rendered, was allowed to retain a certain independence of position until his death in 1908, though he lost control of his militia and his judicial powers were curtailed. With his funeral, say the authors of the traditional history, there ended the monarchy of Porto Novo; his successors, nominated by the governor to carry out restricted administrative functions, retained some social and religious significance for uneducated Gun, but no political authority.[18] In Dahomey as in other coastal colonies the suppression of autonomous African structures was somewhat slower than in the military empire of the Sudan, but in the end it was hardly less effective.

The Imperial Mission

By comparison with the various forms of indirect administration which were to develop in British Africa, the vast territories which in 1895 became officially known as Afrique Occidentale Française saw only few and limited attempts to preserve and work through the structures of African states. The difference is sometimes explained by suggestions that Frenchmen approach colonial policy in a fundamentally different way, that assimilationist ideas represent "profound and constant tendencies of the French people." [19] One need not deny all importance to such ideas, or to certain consequences of their application in Senegal and other parts of the French empire, to suggest that the character of the conquerors, and the urgency with which they eventually moved (to forestall foreigners or to win personal glory), had more to do with the arrangements initially adopted for the government of the new empire. If a Mogho Naba, a King of Abomey, or even a Muslim potentate like Amadu, would cooperate in serving French purposes, no a priori doctrine precluded experiments in this direction; so long as the essential French purpose was simply to exclude British occupation, a protectorate treaty might therefore suffice. But during the 1890s France's demands tended to

[17] Colin W. Newbury, "A Note on the Abomey Protectorate," *Africa* XXIX (1959), 146-55; *The Western Slave Coast and Its Rulers* (Oxford, 1961), pp. 127-33, 180-4.

[18] A. Akindélé and L. Aguessy, *Contribution à l'étude de l'histoire de l'ancien Royaume de Porto-Novo* (Dakar, 1953), pp. 88-90. Cf. Newbury, *Western Slave Coast*, pp. 184-5; Claude Tardits, *Porto Novo* (The Hague, 1958), pp. 55-8, 105.

[19] Hubert Deschamps, "Et maintenant, Lord Lugard?" *Africa*, XXXIII (1963), 296.

become more far-reaching than those which the British made upon African rulers in their sphere. In the Sudan particularly military officers began to feel some sense of imperial purpose which obliged them to rule by methods involving the strictest subordination of all traditional African authorities.

What was this purpose? Critics of imperialism suggest that the ultimate reality was merely the will to dominate or exploit. Certainly French conquest might bring little immediate promise of social improvement. Slavery, which during the nineteenth century had become the great reproach brought against unregenerate Africa by repentant European moralists, was condoned and continued, and not merely in its traditional domestic forms (for which strong pragmatic justification was possible, as even the British had to admit). Village settlements of liberated slaves, established during the conquest of the Sudan with the good intention of providing for refugees who had lost their livelihood as they gained their liberty, became sources of carriers and laborers for the occupying forces; their inhabitants became known locally as "whitemen's slaves." Archinard even gathered recruits for these villages by levying taxes in kind on the internal slave trade, which continued with little effective interference until after 1900.[20] Other "liberated" captives might find themselves assigned as war-booty to France's African allies, or even to the *tirailleurs sénégalais* and their officers. Many acts and practices repugnant to a European conscience followed from France's dependence in many campaigns, on undisciplined auxiliary forces.[21] Even if we exclude as untypical of the French officers psychopaths and sadists like Voulet and Chanoine whose personal atrocities, when revealed, troubled the national conscience,[22] the record of the French "pacification" remains rather brutal. No doubt there were many Africans— those previously in the path of Samori or of Rabeh, a warrior of Arab descent who until his defeat in 1900 was building a new state in the region of Lake Chad—to whom the French appeared as

---

[20] Denise Bouche, "Les Villages de Liberté en A.O.F.," *Bulletin de l'IFAN*, XI (1949), 491-540; XII, 1950, 135-215. For policy toward slavery in a coastal colony, see Colin W. Newbury, "An Early Enquiry into Slavery and Captivity in Dahomey," *Zaïre*, XIV (1960), 53-67.

[21] Paul Vigné [d'Octon], *Au Pays des Fétiches* (Paris, 1890), pp. 70-6. This experience of operations in the Nunez in 1885 turned Vigné, who was a Deputy from 1893-1906, into a firm and vocal anticolonialist.

[22] Jean Suret-Canale, *Afrique Noire*, I (Paris, 1958), 236-44.

liberators; but to others, living in orderly states like Mossi, Futa Jalon, or the central core of Amadu's empire, they must have come as *turbatores rerum*.

But possibly the established order needed to be broken up and transformed. This at least was the conviction of the best of the military leaders, and of French apologies for this new empire. Such men could believe, or at least assume, that French rule would eventually mean the extension to Africa of the secrets of Europe's own prosperity and confidence—economic development, increasing wealth, education which would permit mastery of even the African environment. (Some Frenchmen, fewer than formerly, would still include the extension of Christianity as the greatest blessing of all.) By 1900 the civilian authority of the French Republic had extended its control everywhere except in the desert territories. It now remained to be seen what reality could be given to the French imperial mission.

EIGHT

FRENCH RULE

Colonial rule meant, among other things, the coming of an age of paper. Orthodox historians notoriously live upon paper; yet the colonial period is by no means the best-known section of the African past. Documentation is henceforth produced in plenty; but not all of it is useful, and not all is accessible, to those who seek to understand the transformations of the twentieth century. The difficulties of access are not merely physical ones, imposed by African governments that have inherited the colonial legacy of "fifty year rules"; even more restrictive are the intellectual confines imposed by inherited assumptions or freely assumed commitments. Historical writing on these years is still not plentiful, and much of it is either imperial panegyric, relating every innovation directly or indirectly to the bountiful policies of the colonizers, or invective, more or less seriously documented. Anticolonial writers in their generous indignation, like the apologists, may easily exaggerate the effectiveness of colonial government, for ill in their case rather than for good. Rulers of empires who make high claims for their achievements seem to invite judgment by standards which very few governments could ever hope to satisfy; historical writing about them must thus for a time remain involved in fundamental disagreements about values, where strict neutrality is morally impossible.

Colonial Economies

Figures showing economic development, though difficult to compile and evaluate without bias, may provide the least contentious starting point for discussion of the colonial period. They show some striking though irregular increases in tonnage of vegetable exports in the period between the consolidation of the French empire and the outbreak of World War II. The most spectacular increase is in groundnuts, grown largely in Senegal and Sudan but to a smaller extent in Niger and elsewhere: from under 50,000 tons in 1892 to around 600,000 in 1938. (The bulk of these were still exported unprocessed, not even removed from their husks.) Exports of hardwoods (mostly from Ivory Coast), palm kernels, and to a lesser extent palm oil (largely from Dahomey and Togo) also increased considerably. A temporary boom in rubber exports was reversed before the first war, as the forest resources of Guinea ceased to compete with plantation production elsewhere; but during the interwar years there were clear signs of the success of new crops—cocoa and coffee in Ivory Coast, bananas in Guinea. Persistent attempts to develop cotton production to serve French industries had more modest success, but annual exports of about 4,000 tons were achieved in the 1930s.[1]

There was thus substantial development of that sector of the African economy geared either wholly or in part to production for export markets. The French administration could claim to have encouraged this in several ways: by establishing good order and administrative unity over an extensive area, by providing laws and institutions which favored business activity, by directly providing transport facilities and other pieces of "infrastructure." Before considering these claims, it may be noted that its methods were at least less forceful and disruptive than those employed in parts of French Equatorial Africa during this period. Here early administrators took over remote and impoverished areas, with little established trade and formidable problems of transport, subject to international obligations which restricted their power to raise revenue by the normal method of customs duties on foreign trade. Denied assistance from the French treasury, they sought solutions partly by making arbitrary and often oppressive demands on their subjects, partly by the notorious system of "concessions." Wide economic and governmental powers over large territories were alienated to private companies anxious to make quick profits by extracting natural resources of ivory and rubber (or merely by financial manipulation in Paris). Scandals arose which provoked strong though often isolated protests from conscientious Frenchmen; but the root problem lay less in abuses committed by individuals

---

[1] Full statistical tables would be complicated, and difficult to compile. The figures on which these generalities are based are taken from the secondary works by Thompson and Adloff, Richard-Molard, and Suret-Canale (Vol. II).

than in the conditions under which France assumed these extensive responsibilities.

Even in West Africa, however, the claim that colonial rule brought order is contestable on two counts. Firstly, it exaggerates by implication the disorder of precolonial days; readers should already be aware that many sizeable African states were perfectly capable of administering their lands and maintaining commercial and political relations with their neighbors with much regularity. Secondly, it may exaggerate the success of colonial pacification. It was not until the 1930s that the desert marches were under secure French control; and in other remote areas French control remained precarious. When new burdens were imposed on the Africans, for example during the two world wars, the French *pax* might be disturbed by noncooperation or revolt. These objections are sometimes overstated, innocently or with polemical intent. French rule did not automatically bring increased tranquillity to all West Africans (though it did to many); but it did provide an ordered administrative framework over a vast area, designed to facilitate the movement of goods and persons across ethnic borderlands which might formerly have constituted barriers, and oriented toward French coastal ports. Admittedly, new barriers and disunities were created by the partition (impeding the use of the Gambia river, for example, by territories whose physical and cultural affiliations lay in that direction); but this qualification helps to define the original point. The nature of such development as took place was largely determined by the unification of a particular, somewhat arbitrarily established, group of territories within the new entity, French West Africa.

Within this area, moreover, legislation and policy were designed to encourage a particular pattern of economic development, which, though shaped by Frenchmen, was assumed to be implementing a *pacte coloniale*. Broadly, the intention was to further production by Africans of agricultural and forest produce for export (so far as possible to France) by merchants who would supply in exchange imported consumer goods (so far as possible of French manufacture). Although much more reliance could be placed on market mechanisms than in Equatorial Africa, the government assumed a good deal of responsibility for supervising and assisting these processes. The whole conception is clearly open to many fundamental criticisms of principle, and especially to the charge of having subordinated African development to particular needs of the French economy. There is room for much specialized economic discussion as to whether, given the unstable conditions of international markets, this special relationship with France carried more advantages than drawbacks, and whether any different policies which might conceivably have been adopted in this period would have produced a more efficient distribution of African resources. All that will be done here is to show how certain French policies served this general economic concept, and to demonstrate some of their social or political implications.

As regards land, a most contentious issue in other parts of Africa, reliance upon peasant production involved leaving most of it in African hands. But this did not imply security of tenure for all African occupiers. For one thing French administrators and judges, influenced by concepts of individual ownership derived from Roman law, often gave little recognition to rights held by groups or individuals according to the complexities of African customary law. Lands left fallow under a system of shifting cultivation might be declared unoccupied; and in urban development particularly African rights not registered according to French forms might be arbitrarily disposed of. Secondly, there were cases, covering nearly 200,000 acres by 1939, where long leases of land were conceded to Europeans; these were commonest in Ivory Coast and Guinea, where coffee and bananas respectively were developed to some extent as plantation crops. Thirdly, state forest reserves, not necessarily welcomed by Africans because of the sound conservationist reasons for establishing them, covered a still greater area; and in Ivory Coast rights of commercial exploitation were also commonly conceded, for shorter periods, to European companies.

Acceptance of a market economy implied the use of free labor; economic logic therefore reinforced the ideological commitment against slavery with which the Third Republic undertook its conquests in Africa. It soon became evident that practical difficulties might impede speedy abolition. Not only was domestic slavery almost everywhere still accepted as a necessary, even a stabilizing, feature of traditional society; as already noted, administrative imperatives led the occupying forces in the Sudan to establish their own, not wholly free, labor reserves in the ironically named *villages de liberté*. However, during the first decade of the twentieth century legislation against slavery and slave-dealing was gradually put into effect. At the same time, as in other African colonies, taxation systems were being devised with the aim, not merely of raising revenue, but of inducing Africans to take their labor into the commercial sector of the economy in order to raise the money payments for which they were made responsible. Poll taxes were levied at variable rates; to pay them Senegalese and Sudanese farmers increased their production and sales of groundnuts, Guineans collected rubber from the forest, Dahomeans gathered increased quantities of palm kernels. In the remote forests of upper Guinea the Kissi people, hitherto cut off from contact even with the *dyulas*, began to harvest and sell the kola nuts they had previously neglected, or alternatively to sell their labor to the railway or in the towns.[2]

Such migration, even though no longer directed by slave-traders, was not always wholly voluntary. To bring into the colonial economy distant areas near the limit of the traders' frontier, the French supplemented their taxation system by requiring obligatory labor, in various forms. The labor tax or *prestation* required all adult males to give the government some days unpaid labor (up to twelve in a year), or to commute this obligation to a cash payment. This labor might be used to maintain local roads or do work of some evident value to the village; it might also be used for such distant public purposes as the construction of military airstrips. After 1919, Africans might also be conscripted for paid labor on major public works, such as railway construction, in place of the military service to which they were all legally liable. Apart from these legally sanctioned obligations, French administrators were from time to time induced to use their inevitably powerful influence to recruit labor in heavily populated areas like Mossi for work on private European plantations on the Ivory Coast, often under conditions which were not adequately subjected to administrative inspection or control. In practice the government, convinced that the public interest would be served by the prosperity of these plantations, found itself acting as agent for the compulsory migration of cheap labor. Many Africans died and many suffered through the abuses inherent in this system, which became one of the bitterest grievances of critics of French rule.

What could France show her West African subjects in return for

[2] Yves Person, "Soixante Ans d'évolution en pays Kissi," *CEA* No. 1 (1960), 98-101.

these heavy obligations imposed? Physically, the government could point to a number of transport facilities, water projects, and other public works which European capitalists would not, and Africans could not, have financed. According to an official survey of 1940, public sources had provided over a quarter of the relatively small amount of foreign capital invested in the French African empire;[3] if allowance could be made for the unpaid or underpaid African labor used in the construction of public services, the contribution of the state to the meager capital equipment of French West Africa would appear even more clearly.

Except for two lines eventually nationalized, its railways were built and operated under government direction, utilizing loans of public money. Although plans for a comprehensive network proved over-enthusiastic, four separate systems joined coastal colonies to the savanna; a fairly complex one based on Dakar, serving the main area of groundnut farming; a line from Conakry to Kankan (completed in 1914); one from Abijan to Bouaké (1912), Bobo-Dioulasso (1934) and eventually to Wagadugu; and a Dahomean system, which reached Parakou in 1936. German-built lines in Togo were also extended by the French. The ports which these lines served were developed with public funds. After 1898 Dakar expanded rapidly as an ocean port and naval base; harbor facilities were gradually developed at Cotonou and Conakry; in the 1930s the Ivory Coast's new capital, Abijan, acquired its own new port. With the growing use of automobiles and aircraft in the interwar years, governments used much of the labor they controlled in improving roads and providing airfields, sometimes according to administrative or military, rather than commercial, priorities.

A few projects took colonial governments still further beyond what, in contemporary France, would have been considered their proper role in economic affairs. Much the largest was the establishment in 1932 of the Office du Niger, a public corporation established in association with private companies to develop ambitious irrigation schemes in the middle valley of the Niger. It eventually built a barrage across the river at Sansanding and established agricultural settlements on the reclaimed land; (however, the 25,000 Africans settled by 1955 were vastly fewer than originally contemplated, and

[3] See the official estimates of 1943 (covering Equatorial as well as West Africa) quoted by Suret-Canale, *Afrique Noire*, II, 207.

it is now clear that the scheme is better suited for producing rice than the cotton on which great hopes were originally fixed). Nothing else on such a scale was contemplated in the interwar years; such loans as were granted in the 1930s were designed to assist the ailing metropolitan economy at least as much as to develop the African colonies. However studies were begun for developments in the Senegal valley, and some of these were taken up in the more favorable postwar climate, with the help of the fund known as FIDES. In a less spectacular way, agricultural and veterinary services provided advice, sometimes of much value, to African farmers.

In general French officials saw their purpose as to provide favorable conditions for private entrepreneurs willing to develop African resources, rather than to attempt to develop those resources themselves. This need not imply any close and sinister identity between the personal interests of administrators and capitalists; (in practice relations between them in the field were sometimes rather bad). Liberal assumptions about the natural harmony of interests were still strong enough to convince most administrators that what was good for French business was likely to be good for Africa, at least in the long run. In the short run there were grounds for scepticism. Although in the trading conditions of the interwar years it was not easy for anybody to make a fortune in West Africa, the organization of the market favored the larger expatriate trading companies. The capital at their disposal (though too insignificant to support the theory that the drive to invest was the direct cause of French expansion) gave them a dominant position in the commercial economy, through their capacity, in combination, to regulate buying prices, and their control of facilities for obtaining credit. The main profits of commercial development thus accrued to foreign companies who tended to distribute them as dividends to expatriate stockholders rather than to reinvest them in African development.

These profits were made partly at the expense of Senegalese and other African traders. Such men, lacking the capital and expertise needed to break into direct exportation, simultaneously found their position in internal trade undermined by new competitors. During the last quarter of the nineteenth century Lebanese and Syrians, driven to emigrate by population pressure or Turkish rule, began to find their way, through Marseille, to Senegal and Guinea. In the interwar years their numbers increased and the range of their activities spread; by the mid-1950s their numbers probably approached twenty thousand, more than half of them in Senegal.[4] Their assets included commercial acumen and market sense (first shown in promoting the sales of pink beads called "corals"); communal solidarity; low overhead costs; willingness to accept low income and personal hardship in order to open new markets in remote districts. As they increased their share of the retail trade and commended themselves as buying agents to export merchants, more Africans were squeezed out of their traditional commercial roles. Only the *dyulas*, travelling even farther than the "Syrians" and dealing largely in goods of small export potential (kola, cattle, dried fish), maintained some of their importance in distributive trade.

On closer examination, the advantages to Africans implied by indices of commercial development thus appear rather more dubious. No doubt the Gross National Product of French West Africa, if it could be accurately measured, would be found to have increased, but the benefits were unevenly distributed, geographically and socially. The assumed existence of a *pacte coloniale* was used to induce the production and export to France (albeit on preferential terms) of those primary products which the French economy needed. African farmers found themselves obliged, by market forces reinforced by government policy, to concentrate on a few primary products for which international markets were to prove unstable, especially during the depression of the early 1930s. This specialization, even if it brought some immediate benefits, might involve a decline in subsistence agriculture, to the point where famine could become a seasonal hazard. In the longer run, it could mean overcropping and soil exhaustion. Above all, the system offered little inducement or indeed possibility for Africans to accumulate surpluses and reinvest them in the interest of future production. Even such rudimentary manufacturing processes as the expression of groundnut oil were, until World War II, discouraged, to avoid competition with French industrial interests. The colonial economy provided at best a precarious basis for that social and political progress which Frenchmen hoped would be the fruit of their Imperial mission.

[4] Dates and figures on this subject are unreliable. See the articles by Marwan Hanna in *West Africa* between April 19 and May 24, 1958; also R. Bayly Winder, "The Lebanese in West Africa," *Comparative Studies in History and Society*, IV (1961-62), 296-333.

Social Change

Under colonial rule African society changed in ways which might have been foreseeable but were not all foreseen. Most obviously, there was some acceleration of the movement of peoples toward areas of commercial activity; as has been seen, where the attrition of slavery and the development of a rudimentary labor market failed to produce desired results, governments intervened to bring this about more directly. In a few areas such as Mossi population pressure on inadequate land may also have played a part; but the statistical evidence is too poor to show at what rate, still less for what reasons, African populations increased. It is not even certain how soon colonial medical services were able to offset the impact on the health of Africans of newly imported diseases, such as tuberculosis. European medical science, itself developing rapidly, needed time to understand the special problems of tropical environments; and even as it became clear what needed to be done first priority was given to the special needs of the European residents. Measures to control tropical diseases among African populations, to improve conditions of childbirth and child-rearing, to raise standards of nutrition, were delayed by limitations of finance and manpower.

Precolonial society, of course, had not been immobile; warriors as well as traders had travelled long distances. Under colonial rule the warriors travelled even farther. The approach of World War I led France to rely increasingly on colonial troops to supplement the forces conscripted from her own almost stationary population. The original *tirailleurs sénégalais* were a relatively small force, trained and disciplined primarily (though not exclusively) for African campaigns, mostly recruited in Senegal or Sudan; from 1912 conscription was authorized, and during the war nearly 200,000 men were recruited in A.O.F. They served not only in the conquest of Togo and Cameroun and in repressing insurrections at home, but on such icy killing-grounds as Verdun and the Somme; the official estimate of Africans killed was nearly 25,000. After the war conscription was continued, in the form of selective service for a three-year period; African troops, largely financed by African taxpayers, became a permanent feature of French military policy.

The impact of military service on African society is difficult to assess. The harsh methods of recruitment used in wartime provoked resistance, and a series of insurrections which retained in Africa many of the troops previously raised. In July 1917 Governor-General Van Vollenhoven declared that manpower resources had been drained to the limit of tolerance and that recruitment would have to be suspended. However during 1918 the African Deputy Blaise Diagne, named as Special Commissioner by Clemenceau and accompanied by African officers, was able to recruit some 63,000 men by gentler methods of persuasion, holding out to recruits prospects of training and employment after the war.[5] Veterans were in fact favored by the administration in various ways, and some undoubtedly came to feel loyalty toward France; but for others contact with foreign countries, especially under the traumatic conditions of wartime, destroyed illusions about white superiority and made them seek to change the societies to which they eventually returned. Kissi ex-servicemen, for example, went back to their villages with new skills, new wealth (their military pensions), and above all heightened prestige, due to their experience of dealing with the remote French rulers. The immediate consequence of their return was political unrest; but as new generations of Kissi men enlisted for military service and returned, the veterans became a leading force for modernization within traditional Kissi society.[6] Elsewhere there are signs that the influence of the veterans was more disruptive. In Porto Novo for example they were drawn into a broad current of protest which grouped Muslim dissidents and dynastic opponents of the heirs of Tofa under the leadership of young educated Dahomeans who had established contact with left-wing politicians in France.[7]

The strikes and manifestations of 1923 in southeast Dahomey illustrate the almost platitudinous proposition that social change was most evident in colonial towns. A few of these, like Porto Novo itself and Bamako, grew as extensions of precolonial centers; but the most striking developments were of administrative headquarters, ports or railheads, springing up on sites previously only sparsely settled. The civic life of such towns was in many respects dominated by the Europeans who controlled commerce, or the colonial govern-

---

[5] I am grateful to Mr. Michael Crowder for showing me some of the results of his researches in the archives of AOF at Dakar into wartime recruitment. With Mr. Wesley Johnson, Mr. Crowder plans to publish a study of this subject shortly.

[6] Person, CEA No. 1, pp. 90, 106-7.

[7] John Ballard, "The Porto Novo Incidents of 1923; Politics in the Colonial Era," Odu, II (1965), 52-75.

ment, and who took their families in increasing numbers as twentieth-century developments in tropical medicine made it safe to do so. Dakar, administrative and economic capital of French West Africa, had over 10,000 European inhabitants in 1934; by 1951 its population of 250,000 included 22,000 Europeans and 4,500 Syrians and Lebanese.[8] In the first decades after its settlement in 1857 Dakar had grown only slowly, for Rufisque proved a better center for exporting groundnuts; but public money improved Dakar's port and railway facilities and from the end of the century, when it was selected for development as capital of French West Africa and as a naval base, it expanded very rapidly.[9] With its striking contrasts in housing and living standards, its cosmopolitan facilities and great public buildings, Dakar has often seemed to exist for the benefit of Frenchmen rather than Africans; but like other colonial towns, it has simultaneously provided the environment in which a new, lively, differentiated African society could develop.

Urbanization has recently become a popular subject for social research of many varieties. Studies carried out in African towns, including many in French-speaking Africa, have produced findings with wide implications for historians. Only two extremely general points will be made here.[10] First, and obviously, urbanization means change. For individuals this involves taking "new bearings, forming new social ties of an unfamiliar kind, and acquiring new values with reference both to material conditions and social relations." For society as a whole it implies the formation of new groups and associations, for the purposes of work, recreation, worship, mutual assistance, and political action. These changes may, and in many opinions must, be understood as aspects of the emergence of new social classes, created by the new shape of the economy. In Marxist terms, the classes which developed during the colonial period may be described as a petite bourgeoisie (junior civil servants, commercial clerks and agents, market traders and shopkeepers, urban landlords, letter-writers, journalists, school teachers, headed by a small elite of pro-

---

[8] Richard-Molard, *op. cit.*, p. 215.

[9] Roger Pasquier, "Villes du Sénégal au xix⁰ siècle," *Revue française d'histoire d'Outre-Mer*, Nos. 168-9 (1960), 387-426.

[10] They are made in light particularly of the conference report on "Urbanization in African Social Change," privately published in 1963 by the Centre of African Studies, University of Edinburgh. The following quotation is from Daryll Forde's paper "Background and Approaches," p. 2.

fessional men) and a proletariat (port and railway workers, building laborers and tradesmen, domestic servants, porters and casual laborers, with a sizeable fringe of family dependents having no regular employment). Both "classes" are still relatively small; even in the early 1950s the number of wage-earners in French West Africa was estimated at 350,000 or 2% of the population.[11]

But secondly, these changes do not produce any sharp and sudden cleavage between urban and rural society. Migration is a continuing and two-way process; the new groupings in towns are superimposed upon families, households, and "tribal" associations which maintain close links with traditional ways of life and with particular villages and families. Along these channels new ideas and expectations are disseminated into the countryside. The towns can thereby influence the vastly greater section of the population which, though affected with varying intensity by commercial development and government policy, remains essentially rural in domicile and outlook.

Changing Beliefs

In religion, one apparent characteristic of the period has been that animist systems of belief and ritual have proved inadequate as guides through the problems of social change and have lost ground to the universal religions of Christianity, Islam, and secular humanism. Less obvious but even more general has been a tendency for these universal religions to become naturalized in Africa through interpenetration with traditional cults and beliefs. Government policy, by encouraging missionary education, tended to encourage the spread of orthodox Christianity. Although subsidies to church schools from public funds were restricted after France separated church from state in 1905, Catholic and Protestant missions could still enjoy fiscal and legal privileges, and might even be favored by governors known in France for strong lay principles. This collaboration was encouraged not only by the government's need to tap all possible sources of teachers and funds, but by the conviction of many (not all) administrators and missionaries that African conditions demanded a specially close relationship between church and state. At an early stage in the occupation of the Sudan a French officer, noting how at Kita the Holy Ghost Fathers were instilling in young Mandinka

[11] Thomas L. Hodgkin, *Nationalism in Colonial Africa* (London, 1956), p. 118.

pupils a sense of France's power and greatness, declared that in such circumstances it was the duty of all good Frenchmen, regardless of their religious convictions, to turn out for Mass;[12] practical Erastianism like this ensured that even under the Republican flag Christian missions were encouraged to expand their schools, and also their spiritual influence. Their success has been moderate, or rather localized. Figures of religious allegiance are even more difficult to evaluate than most African statistics; but by 1953 the Catholics claimed 630,410 converts and Protestant churches 116,154. Up to a quarter of the Catholics and a third of the Protestants were in Togo; not only were Protestant missions well established before the French occupation, but their expansion after 1918 was facilitated by provision for religious equality in the terms of the French mandate of 1919.[13] Protestant churches previously established also progressed under French administration in southern Dahomey, and a number of small but highly evangelical missions were allowed to begin work in inland districts previously untouched by Christianity.

During the twentieth century European and American Christians have begun to distinguish more clearly between universally valid truths of the Christian Gospel and certain ethical teachings, liturgical practices, and institutional forms which, though deeply rooted in the traditions of their own churches, it is no longer judged essential or expedient to transmit overseas. This understanding has been slowly and painfully achieved; the establishment of genuine dialogue between Africans and Europeans has been little easier in ecclesiastical than in political matters. The Catholic church, cautious and slow in ordaining African clergy before the second world war, may thereby have limited its access to adult African minds; among Protestants, in Africa as in Europe, dissent has sometimes expressed itself in heresy or separatism. Not included in the statistical claims of the missionary churches, but making their own contribution toward a symbiosis of African and European beliefs, are the adherents of a wide range of smaller churches or sects, heretical or schismatic from an orthodox standpoint, "syncretic" in the language of modern

[12] M. Etienne Péroz, Au Niger (Paris, 1894), pp. 339-43.
[13] Thompson and Adloff, op. cit., p. 585; cf. J. Spencer Trimingham, The Christian Church and Islam in West Africa (London, 1955), p. 54; Robert Cornevin, Histoire du Togo (Paris, 1959), pp. 309, 325. The text of the Cameroun mandate is in Buell, Native Problem, II, 374-77; the Togo mandate is similar.

social analysts. They are probably best regarded as the attempts of men perplexed by rapid change to ground within the Old Testament of animist traditions truths which they have perceived within the Christian Gospel of the missionaries. Thus Prophet W. W. Harris, a Methodist-educated preacher of Liberian birth, was inspired by a vision of Gabriel to undertake a ministry of baptism in the southern Ivory Coast in the years 1913-15, which eventually won over 100,000 followers. Orthodox missionaries suspicious of heresy and administrators suspicious of novelty were equally puzzled by this man who aroused dangerously intense emotional excitement yet preached hard work and obedience to established authority; who condoned polygamy and other "pagan" practices while denouncing theft, drunkenness, adultery, Sabbath-breaking, and animist rites of worship with enviable effectiveness. Harris's repatriation to Liberia during World War I did not destroy his work; he had in a sense given the Ivory Coast its first national church, "founded by an African for Africans." Some of his congregations later provided a solid foundation for orthodox Methodism in the Ivory Coast; others remained independent in organization and doctrine, or followed other prophets who departed further from the Christian traditions of Europe.[14]

For Muslims, the process by which a universal religion may become "naturalized" and modified in an African environment was not unfamiliar; similar processes seem to have characterized the first, though not the second, phase of Islamic expansion in West Africa. French rule now inaugurated a third great forward movement. This may seem surprising; despite the persistent ambivalence in French official attitudes (especially notable in the career of Faidherbe) many administrators saw strong reasons for hostility to Islam. Muslim rulers had offered the strongest resistance to France's conquest of West Africa; French interests in North Africa and the Middle East gave her reasons to fear any movement which might unite Muslims against European Christians; the Republic had not abandoned its alliance with Christianity in Africa, and in any case hardened anticlericals might find the influence of *marabouts* even more pernicious than that of priests. Administrators wrote of "the peril of Islam," and some-

---

[14] The most recent account of Harris and his movement is at pp. 259-78 of the monumental survey by Bohumil Holas of *Le Séparatisme réligieux en Afrique Noire: l'exemple de la Côte d'Ivoire* (Paris, 1965). This contains good bibliographical references.

times tried to counter it by encouraging animist revivals; scholarly officials like Paul Marty undertook research, with the ulterior motive of identifying possible troublespots; zealots like the Hamallists, an unorthodox sect of the Tijaniyya in northwest Sudan, were subject to official suspicion and harassment. Yet under French rule Islam expanded in every territory, and consolidated its predominance in Senegal, Sudan, and Guinea as well as Mauritania and Niger. Informed observers concluded that "with true liberal obstinacy" the administration was encouraging this growth.[15]

Some of the reasons for expansion lie in the social consequences of French rule rather than its conscious purposes. Improved communications assisted the movement of proselytizing Muslims by land and sea; pilgrimages to Mecca, impeded during the nineteenth century by political upheavals on the overland route, could now be made by modern transportation (by those who could afford it). Many conversions took place in the new towns; mosques offered centers of cohesion and fellowship from which immigrants could begin the process of adjustment to urban life. In such places as Mossi the authority of animist rulers formerly resistant to Islam was undermined. Muslim law, more easily comprehensible by Europeans than animist custom, tended increasingly to influence decisions of the colonial judiciary. And as their knowledge improved French administrators might come to recognize some community of interests with leading *marabouts*, and so, especially in Senegal, to reinforce their authority.

The oustanding example is provided by the Muridiyya, a Qadiri *tarikh* practicing the cult of saints which was founded among the Wolof in 1886 by Ahmed Bamba (c. 1850-1927) a kinsman of the *damel* Lat-Dior; it now claims 400,000 followers. Its leaders completed the Islamization of the Wolof by methods which have been described as "the Wolofization of Islam": as in the Harrisite movement, orthodox doctrines were accommodated to traditional beliefs with striking effects. At the same time the call of the leaders for financial contributions coincided felicitously with opportunities for extending groundnut cultivation provided by railway construction. New lands in Senegal were colonized under the leadership of Murid *marabouts*; Islam, Wolof influence, and the "traders' frontier" expanded together in

---

[15] Richard-Molard, *op. cit.*, p. 87; for Hamallism, see Alphonse Gouilly, *L'Islam dans l'A.O.F.* (Paris, 1952), pp. 126-61.

peaceful substitution for armed *jihad*. The French, who showed their initial suspicion by twice exiling Ahmed Bamba and during the period 1895-1907, came to see merit in a sect which undertook commercial development without resisting their authority; with their acquiescence and encouragement the Murid leaders at the great new mosque of Touba built up religious influence and considerable worldly wealth.[16]

In West Africa, Islam remained largely conservative and traditional. Apart from the Ahmadiyya, a Shi-ite sect from Pakistan which has only marginally influenced French-speaking territories, the agents of its expansion were little influenced by those modernizing intellectual tendencies which have become important in the Middle East. African Koranic schools, until after the second war at least, remained largely apart from the modern sector of the educational system, although the administration made some attempts to draw together French and Arabic education at higher levels. Individual Muslim leaders have of course acquired modern education and outlooks (especially since 1945, when some have attended Middle Eastern universities); but among the intellectual leadership as a whole it seems that the influence of Islam, and to a lesser extent of Christianity, had tended to be overshadowed by the growing appeal of secular, science-based, humanism. Even here, however, a process of "naturalization" may be observed; African intellectuals seem almost unanimously to reject philosophical materialism, basing their humanism on concepts of human solidarity and spiritual unity which they discern within traditional African cosmologies. Paradoxically, this call to return to African values has been most clearly articulated by graduates of a colonial educational system largely assimilationist in conception.

Western Education and African Culture

As everywhere in Africa, western-type education was recognized by the French administration as one of the most important motors for change, even though it has not always driven society in exactly the direction intended. French educational purposes were summarized by Governor-General Carde in 1924 as the instruction of the mass and the formation of an elite. But although the administrative structure of a state educational system had been enacted in 1903, the actual

---

[16] See Vincent Monteil, *L'Islam Noir* (Paris, 1964), pp. 265-71; Gouilly, *op. cit.*, pp. 116-25.

provision of adequate schools for the masses was delayed by deficiencies in money, men, and understanding. The number of school places
long remained small. Excluding Koranic schools there were about
15,000 children in school in A.O.F. in 1910, 70,000 in 1938, and 130,-
000 in 1949, plus 40,000 in Togo. (Approximately 20% of the places
for A.O.F. were in Catholic or Protestant mission schools.) The 1949
figures may represent about 6% of school-age population in A.O.F.
and 27% in Togo.[17] The distribution of these limited opportunities
was uneven; in particular the village schools which provided the essential first step of a child's educational ladder were sparsely and un-
evenly available. Already by 1907 there were 33 regional schools, providing the second stage of primary education in two-thirds of the
administrative *cercles* of A.O.F., but only 76 village schools; by 1935
there were about 80 regional schools with 23,321 pupils, but only
about 300 village schools with 29,294 pupils.[18] Although education
was in principle open to all without fees, the vast majority of children
still had no school available. A child's chance of obtaining education
in coastal Senegal, or in missionary strongholds like southern Dahomey ("the Latin Quarter of West Africa," and source of many of
its clerks, teachers, and journalists) were far higher than elsewhere.

Besides these limitations in quantity, numerous criticisms have been
(justly or unjustly) made about the quality of primary instruction.
Financial and physical limitations delayed the recruitment and training of a true elementary teaching profession. Whereas in English-
speaking territories, mission schools employed Sierra Leoneans and
other educated Africans, Senegalese *habitants* rarely filled this role.
In the first years of French rule French N.C.O.s or customs-men often
ran village schools; later the system relied heavily on inexperienced
African monitors. When European teachers were available their
teaching was often accused of being irrelevantly harnessed to the
French educational system and French literary culture; consequent
reactions in favor of practical agricultural or vocational training might
lead to children being set to unskilled labor, possibly for the benefit
of the schoolmaster or commandant. There were also linguistic prob-

[17] Figures from the summary in Lord Hailey, *An African Survey, Revised 1956*
(London, 1957), pp. 1193-1203, 1260. Detailed calculations on Togo school
attendance are in Cornevin, *Togo*, pp. 332-34. A very useful analysis of conditions
in the 1920s is Buell, *Native Problem*, II, 49-64.
[18] Suret-Canale, *Afrique Noire*, II, 468; Thompson and Adloff, *French West
Africa*, pp. 518, 523.

lems. Colonial and mission schools (except in Togo) used French as the language of instruction from the start of primary schooling; attempts to teach in Wolof were abandoned as early as 1829. The problems of mastering a foreign language from the start of schooling made for high dropout rates; even in Senegal in 1960, after 130 years' experience of instruction in French, fewer than a third of the children entering primary school successfully completed their studies, and many were still repeating French phrases with little comprehension of meaning.[19]

French-speaking Africans who won their way through the elementary schools and the more selective higher primary schools (*écoles primaires supérieures*) might be better prepared than British protected persons educated in a vernacular language to proceed to secondary education on an equal footing with Europeans; but their opportunities for doing so were by no means equal. The limited provisions for African secondary education in French West Africa were primarily designed to provide administration and business with competent employees of intermediate rank and status; they consisted of technical trade schools, teacher colleges, institutions for training interpreters and functionaries somewhat in the tradition of Faidherbe's *Ecole des Otages*. The most selective of the federal colleges, the Ecole Normale William Ponty, produced teachers, officials, candidates for further training as dispensers and medical auxiliaries, of intellectual distinction and vocational competence; but its standards and qualifications were only gradually and partially assimilated to those of metropolitan France. Subsidized study overseas, as formerly practiced in Senegal, was discouraged by the government-general after a few Africans, sent to the *école normale* at Aix in the early 1920s, were judged to have acquired subversive ideas. But the professed ideal of educating Africans and Frenchmen to the same level of universalist civilization was practiced on a tiny scale in Senegal. Here the rapid growth of the resident European population at last created an effective demand for local secondary schools. The school at Saint-Louis became a French *lycée* in 1920, that at Dakar in 1940. Though primarily run for Euro-

[19] David Hapgood, "Sub-Saharan Education and Rural Development" in William H. Lewis (ed.), *French-Speaking Africa* (New York, 1965), pp. 121-23; cf. above, p. 85. See also Denise Bouche, "Les écoles françaises au Soudan à l'époque de la conquête, 1884-1900," *CEA*, No. 22 (1966).

pean children, they had no color-bar; qualified children of African families were admitted, and in 1946, 174 of the 723 pupils in the two schools were classified as African.[20] From here a narrow gate was open to French higher education and genuine equality of status, though it was passed only by a few Senegalese. By 1945 the educated elite of French West Africa included, besides 2,000 or so alumni of Ponty and the *Ecole de médecine,* a few lawyers and veterinarians who had returned from France and a single, and justly celebrated, African *professeur agrégé,* born in Joal but long resident in France—the future President Senghor.

Theorists who saw as the goal of colonial policy the extension to Africa of the "blessings of civilization" and the cultural heritage of western Europe had always been most numerous in France. Now the process of cultural assimilation, which had so long operated in the microcosm of Senegal, seemed to be bearing first fruits—promising in quality, though few in number—from the extended West African empire. Representatives of empires which had followed different policies applauded the apparent success with which "Africans learn to be French." [21] This notion of exporting European civilization to Africa, though less fashionable today, was often exceedingly well intentioned, and not invariably naïve in conception. But—apart from reiterating the small scale on which it was practiced—two major comments may be made about its operation. During the past century, science and technological skill have come to form an increasingly large part—and one particularly relevant to the problems of developing countries—of that heritage of "European civilization" which assimilationists wish to transfer to Africa. This new learning, still very imperfectly absorbed into the minds and educational systems of Europeans, has in general been still less effectively transmitted overseas. This point is made in general terms and needs to be qualified by more detailed study. As far as syllabuses are concerned, it might prove that the French have been rather more adaptable than the British; their training of medical auxiliaries may be an example. At another level, it would be possible to draw up impressive lists of research work inaugurated by numerous

[20] Thompson and Adloff, *op. cit.,* p. 538.
[21] Title of the very favorable report which W. B. Mumford and G. St. J. Orde Browne published after a survey of education in French West Africa in 1935.

bodies in France and Africa (notably by the *Institut Français d'Afrique Noire*, founded in 1938, and its predecessor the Committee of Historical and Scientific Studies); and of successful applications of agricultural, medical, and engineering science to specific African problems. But a strong impression remains that French as well as British educational policy often tended to equate "civilization" with a literary and philosophical culture less directly related to concrete social needs.

Secondly, that culture has sometimes been intruded at the expense of devaluing authentic African experience and tradition. It is not accidental that the strongest movement to reassert Africa's cultural identity has come from that elite who used the opportunities of assimilative education most effectively. Initially this reaction might actually be led by Europeans; it was not necessary to be an African to find it ludicrous that Guinean schoolchildren should be taught about their ancestors, the Gauls. Some dedicated French teachers at Ponty sympathetically encouraged their pupils to express their own cultural experience in such forms as art, dance, and drama. But paternalist administrators, often influenced by nineteenth-century racial theories, were usually less happy in their attempts to define the identity of Negro African culture. "The Negro spirit," wrote one early African romantic,

> is something like the spirit of our first ancestors. It is unpolished and crude, but its freshness is without comparison. In coming into contact with it, one feels humble but also immersed in the very sources of human sensitivity. Singular antithesis, this contact makes one at the same time less proud and more virile! [22]

For the small but growing educated elite, a cultural role based on animal sensuality was hardly satisfying. Young Africans, while recognizing the attractions of French civilization, and of the prizes which success in colonial society could offer, felt the need to express and reinterpret authentic African experiences independently of European patronage. In 1935 a young Senegalese, Ousmane Socé Diop, published a novel, *Karim*, which explores some of the problems of African *evolués* in the *civilisation métisse* of Dakar. His young men

---

[22] Pacquier, "Sur l'âme noire," *Dépêche Coloniale*, June 3, 1902, quoted R. F. Betts, *Assimilation and Association in French Colonial Theory, 1890-1914* (N.Y., 1961).

hesitated to break finally with the old Senegal in order to espouse European customs, although some of these imposed themselves. Their hearts spoke in favor of ancestral tradition, their interests in favor of the practical modern outlook of the West.

When Karim finally returns to his girl in Saint-Louis he symbolically resumes Senegalese dress; but his European clothes are not rejected, simply laid aside as inappropriate to this environment: "it was as singular to wear a *boubou* in European-dressed company as to put on a tight and dowdy jacket-suit in a society that wore Muslim dress." [23]

This sensible and pragmatic compromise did not satisfy all the young leaders of the interwar generation. But whereas assertions of African cultural identity might be applauded by liberal Europeans, political manifestations were highly suspect to colonial administrators. In the 1930s young Ivoirians received some encouragement for their attempts to found an African theater, but the first African newspaper in the Ivory Coast had to be sponsored by a Senegalese citizen under cover of his favored legal status. Other political protests—like those of Louis Hunkanrin in Dahomey in the 1920s—originated in Paris, sometimes under the protection of French radical movements like the League of the Rights of Man (which *were* allowed to found branches in the colonies).[24] But it was again in the search for cultural identity, rather than in political protest, that Negro expatriates in Paris achieved their most lasting influence. This was exercised by a largely West Indian group with one outstanding Senegalese member, Senghor.

Senghor's career offers interesting material for comparison with the political struggles of English-speaking contemporaries like Kenyatta and Nkrumah. Son of a well-to-do Sérère businessman in the old Catholic town of Joal, educated initially by the Holy Ghost Fathers at nearby N'gazobil, Senghor began his higher studies in Paris in 1928, at the age of 22 (entering the same class in the prestigious Lycée Louis-le-Grand as de Gaulle's future premier, Georges Pompidou). He had a distinguished career at the Sorbonne and in 1933 became the first African *professeur agrégé*. To receive the degree he had to become naturalized as a French citizen; having done so he was received with military honors on his return to Dakar. But shortly he

---

[23] Ousmane Socé, *Karim: Roman sénégalais* (Paris, 1948), pp. 105, 145.
[24] F. J. Amon d'Aby, *La Côte d'Ivoire dans la Cité africaine* (Paris, 1951), pp. 62-66, 154-63. John Ballard, "The Porto Novo Incident." See above, p. 122.

returned to France, to a post in a provincial *lycée*; to war service, a German prison camp, service in the Resistance; to a growing reputation as a poet and authority on the French language. While retaining his roots in Catholicism he joined the French Socialist party and gave adult education classes in French to the workers of Tours. His career seemed a model of how Africans could be assimilated to French culture. In fact Senghor, as a student in the early 1930s, was struggling to reconcile the cerebral appeal of European rationalism and the aesthetic power of European art with more intuitive and sensory insights into spiritual reality which he found in traditional African cultures, and which were being acknowledged by Europeans like Picasso, André Breton, and later Sartre. In close fellowship with Aimé Césaire and other young intellectuals from the French West Indies, Senghor explored the dilemmas of Negroes tempted to renounce their origins for the rewards of accepting assimilation; met Afro-American leaders of the "Harlem Renaissance" and translated their poetry; because aware of the cultural ferment taking place in Haiti and the importance attached to Africa by its leader, Price-Mars. Together Cesaire and Senghor produced a journal, *L'Etudiant Noir* (of which no copies appear to have survived); in poetry, prose, and conversation they explored the nature of Africa's cultural personality, seeking to give meaning and weight, in the eyes of the world, to the distinctively African values of *négritude*. In their excellent French they expressed the same sort of protest against the suffocating effects of close adherence to European forms as Harris had voiced in the less articulate language of religious separatism.[25]

Colonial Government

In governmental structure even more than in educational policy, France's supposed assimilationist tradition was given only a limited and strictly defined application in the period after the conquest. In the Senegalese towns political rights which had lapsed under the

---

[25] I am much indebted to the brief biography of Senghor in the useful introduction to his work by Armand Guibert, *Léopold Sédar Senghor* (Paris, 1962). The key documents of negritude are to be found in Senghor's *Anthologie de la nouvelle poésie nègre et malgache de langue française* (Paris, 1948). Senghor's later writings are too numerous to list here. There is useful intellectual background in Abiola Irele, "Negritude or Black Cultural Nationalism," *JMAS*, III (1965), 321-48, and in Lilyan Kesteloot, *Les Ecrivains noirs de langue française* (Bruxelles, 1963).

Second Empire were revived in the early years of the Third Republic. Elective municipal communes were set up in Saint-Louis and Gorée in 1872, in Rufisque and Dakar a few years later; by 1879 citizens of these four towns had also regained the right to elect a *Conseil-Général*, and one Deputy to the French National Assembly. This legislation was framed primarily to guarantee to resident Frenchmen and mulattoes the full rights of citizenship, but it applied to all *originaires* —that is, to men of all races and backgrounds born in the four communes. From the point of view of African rights it was implemented in the nick of time. Once the territorial expansion of the 1880s was under way Frenchmen realized that literal application of the principle of equal rights for all French subjects would produce a vast electoral bloc of African Muslims and animists, knowing no French and incapable in any foreseeable future of participating purposefully in discussion of the problems of colonial society. The danger was underlined by the political development of the communes. African voters were quickly enlisted by European merchants or mulatto political leaders, who, increasingly at odds with colonial administrators, developed much skill in manipulating the unsophisticated electorate, and in legitimizing factious intrigues with such demagogic slogans as "Senegal for the Senegalese." [26] Attempts by indignant governors to annul the voting rights of African *originaires* were rejected by French courts, but the franchise was held to be restricted to men born in the commune where they sought to exercise it. *Originaires*, unless specifically naturalized, were thus treated as subjects with special, localized privileges; lest they should establish a claim to extend these, they were actually prevented from subjecting themselves to French conscription laws.

Yet even these vestigial assimilationist institutions proved a bridgehead capable of extension. In 1914 Blaise Diagne, an African customs official with wide experience of the French empire and of moderate anticolonial activity, was elected Deputy, with broad support among African electors, thus breaking the political monopoly of Frenchmen and mulattoes. Two years later, in return for his services in recruiting soldiers for the French army, Diagne secured the passage of a law declaring that *originaires* of the four communes were indeed French

[26] Louis Sonolet, *L'Afrique Occidentale française* (Paris, 1912), pp. 13-5. Pierre Mille, "The 'Black Vote' in Senegal," *Journal of the African Society*, I (1901), 64-79. See above, p. 86.

citizens, exempt from the special burdens imposed on French subjects
and entitled to do their military service on the same basis as Frenchmen, even if they elected to remain subject to Muslim private law.
There were 25,000 such citizens in 1921, and nearly 80,000 by 1936.
An additional small door to French citizenship had been opened in
1912. Literate and well-behaved Africans who had distinguished themselves in French service could become naturalized by furnishing elab-
orate proofs of cultural assimilation, and accepting the full obligations
of French public and private law. Up to 1922, 94 West Africans took
advantage of this procedure. In 1937, when the number had risen to
about 2,000, the conditions for naturalization were eased slightly; but
it remained clear that legal assimilation would not be practiced on
any considerable scale.[27]

From the 1890s therefore some Frenchmen began to speak of a
"policy of association" as a preferable alternative to the cultural or
legal assimilation of the new empire they were acquiring. The influence of anthropological thought about the diversity of cultures (usually mixed up with quasi-evolutionary theories about the inequality of
races) was reinforced by lessons drawn from empirical observation of
Dutch and British colonies. Frenchmen might now be urged to respect the individuality of African institutions, cooperating with the
"natural rulers" and protecting them against the newly-apparent perils
of assimilation into colonial society. This was an attitude for which
antecedents could be found in the policies of Faidherbe and Gallieni,
and which could to some extent actually be applied in the protected
states of Indo-China and the Maghreb. But in West Africa the
classe dirigeante which Lyautey aimed to discover had been largely
and deliberately destroyed during the conquest, and the process continued in the years which followed. Treaties which it had suited
France to sign during the international scramble were unilaterally
repudiated; historic states were carved up into administrative *cantons*.
At this level (and to a lesser degree at that of the village) chiefs,
whether or not they could claim to be legitimate inheritors of precolonial authority, became agents of native administration—a branch
of the colonial bureaucracy, almost ripe for unification like the federal

[27] Buell, *op. cit.*, I, 946-57; Michael Crowder, *Senegal* (London, 1962), pp.
16-22; Hailey, *An African Survey* (London, 1957), pp. 338-9. I am particularly
indebted to Mr. G. Wesley Johnson for a prepublication view of his important
paper on Blaise Diagne, since published in *Africa*, XXXVI (1966), 235-52.

veterinary service. The term *association* became carelessly or sophistically used to cover a variety of improvised procedures and institutions in which ultimate power became increasingly concentrated in the hands of the new French rulers—much as a horse may be associated with its rider. Blunter Frenchmen preferred to reject a term which could seem to imply equality of status, and to describe French policy as one of "benevolent tutelage." [28]

While the chiefs were turned into subordinate agents for the execution of French policies, the position of their subjects was even more tightly controlled. Constitutionally the supreme authority in A.O.F. was the Governor-General, and under him the colonial Governors, subject to the imperfectly effective control of the Republic in Paris; except to some extent in the four communes of Senegal, Africans had little prospect of asserting personal rights against them. French subjects (as distinct from citizens) were not under the jurisdiction of French courts but of an improvised system of *justice indigène*. Half-hearted attempts to preserve and develop native courts were soon abandoned; instead French administrators, assisted by African assessors, dispensed civil and criminal justice, theoretically according to local law and custom. But African customs were diverse, imperfectly accessible to Europeans (the first authoritative publication of *Coutumiers juridiques de l'A.O.F.* was in 1939), and in any case destined to change in the colonial situation. Nor was there any penal code to control the severity of disciplinarian commandants. Beyond the constituted courts, a much-hated system known as the *indigénat*, first developed in Algeria, authorized acts of administrative tyranny. Governors were authorized to define certain types of offense by decree, administrative officers to try such offenses summarily and (within limits) to fine, imprison, or deport without possibility of appeal or judicial review. The *indigénat*, together with the systems of taxation, conscription, and forced labor, made many of France's African subjects as heavily dependent on the will of those who held them in tutelage as they had formerly been on the will of their chiefs. Little benevolence could be expected by any who showed signs of rebelliousness or independence.

[28] Sonolet, *L'Afrique Occidentale française*, pp. 29-30. Two recent discussions are Raymond F. Betts, *Assimilation and Association in French Colonial Theory, 1890-1914* (New York, 1961); M. D. Lewis, "The Assimilation Theory in French Colonial Policy," *Comparative Studies in Society and History*, IV (1962), 129-53.

Some Frenchmen, appreciating the defects of the system, aimed to improve it. Between 1909 and 1917 Governors Ponty and Van Vollenhoven spoke of rehabilitating natural rulers, reconstituting the most serviceable elements in traditional society, making "association" a reality. They began to suspect that the strength and originality of African institutions had been underrated; that some who had been presented as representative authorities for investment as village chiefs were really men of straw, designed to shield the real chief whose authority was still recognized by the people and by the country societies. In the 1920s Maurice Delafosse, an administrator who was also a pioneer of African studies, tried to import Lugardian doctrines to the *Ecole Coloniale,* urging administrative cadets to "safeguard native institutions, make them evolve slowly in their natural *cadre,* avoid creating caricatures of Europe." But his success seems to have been only moderate; it was difficult to eradicate an already established administrative style of treating chiefs as subordinate functionaries. Despite experiments in appointing local "Councils of Notables," French policy between the wars seems to have evolved less by strengthening the role of "native authorities" in government than by limited extensions of civic rights. Chiefs, ex-servicemen and Africans who had "evolved" into a certain status in colonial society were exempted from the *indigénat,* without necessarily acquiring citizenship; twenty-three towns became "mixed communes," with appointed Mayors and councils elected on colorblind, though restricted, franchises; reliable Africans were appointed—later, indirectly elected—to advisory *conseils d'administration* in Ivory Coast, Guinea, Dahomey, and Sudan, and to an advisory council for the whole federation. In Senegal the *conseil-général* was in 1920 replaced by a Colonial Council on which French citizens of all races were represented along with chiefs (the latter being more reliable from the administration's point of view).[29] The effect of these mild moves in the direction of assimilationist principles

[29] For the Colonial Council, Buell, *op. cit.,* I, 967-82. For recent discussion of French policy, Hubert Deschamps, "Et Maintenant, Lord Lugard?" *Africa,* XXXIII (1963); Michael Crowder, "Indirect Rule—French and British Style," *Africa,* XXXIV (1964).

In Togo (that portion of the former German colony placed under French mandate in 1919) the institutions of French rule were broadly similar, but conscription was not enforced, and a penal code was introduced. Although after 1934 France began to integrate the administration with that of Dahomey, Togolese spokesmen retained a sense of separate identity and to some extent of privileged status.

was of course limited by the relatively meager opportunities for economic or educational evolution available to Africans in this interwar period. Postwar critics of French colonialism could still point to a "pattern" of an underlying assimilationist theory contrasting with a reality too often made up of a small indigenous *elite,* itself largely subordinated to the predominantly metropolitan *citoyen,* and a large indigenous mass which remained substantially in the cadres of its own culture, economy, and law.[30]

There are obvious respects in which the French colonial empire may be sharply distinguished from its British rival—professed aims of policy, institutions of government, cultural assumptions, administrative "style." Such contrasts have often been discussed, and will not be enlarged upon here. Less evident perhaps are the similarities imposed by the colonial situation itself, by realities unavoidable by Europeans exercising power in West Africa during the early decades of the twentieth century. Both powers were constrained—by the parsimony of metropolitan Parliaments, the scarcity in Africa of money and skilled men, the unsettled conditions of African societies suddenly faced with the onset of Europe—to devise systems of government which would concentrate immediate administrative control in the hands of agents on whom they could rely. At the grass roots, both empires were governed by authoritarian paternalism, checked by the sense of responsibility of the man on the spot—the district commissioner or *commandant de cercle.* In neither system was there any doubt about the ultimate authority of the administrative officer, as distinct from the proper manner for the exercise of his authority. As Van Vollenhoven concluded a circular (intended to improve the standing of chiefs within African society) "there are not two authorities in the *cercle,* the French authority and the native authority— there is only one. Only the *commandant de cercle* commands; only he is responsible. The native chief is only an instrument, an auxiliary." [31] Lugard had previously defined the underlying assumption of British Indirect Rule in these terms:

[30] Kenneth Robinson, *The Public Law of Overseas France Since the War* (Oxford, 1950).
[31] Van Vollenhoven circular, Aug. 15, 1917, quoted P. Alexandre, *Le Problème des chefferies en Afrique noire française.* (*La Documentation française,* No. 2508, 1959).

There are not two sets of rulers—British and native—working either separately or in co-operation, but a single Government in which the native chiefs have well-defined duties and an acknowledged status equally with British officials. Their duties should never conflict, and should overlap as little as possible. They should be complementary to each other, and the chief himself must understand that he has no right to place and power unless he renders his proper services to the State.[32]

The difference in emphasis is notable, but so is the underlying agreement as to the ultimate seat of power.

The administrators themselves might not have welcomed the comparison. National pride tended to produce unfavorable images of the foreign administrator. French officers were assumed by British countries to be deceitful, sympathetic to slavery, debauchers of African women; they in turn believed British administrators to be held aloof from their subjects by overindulgence in tea, golf, and polo.[33] And certainly there were differences in the cultural background and assumptions of French and British officials. The French were indeed semiofficially encouraged to extend the old tradition of *mariage à la mode du pays* to the interior by taking African mistresses for a whole tour of service; the advantages (in the order stated) were that they would avoid syphilitic prostitutes; establish "bonds of sympathy" with chiefly families; avoid the temptation to rape the wives of their African subordinates; form sentimental attachments which might serve as a prophylactic against alcoholism; and learn something of African languages, customs, and "the black soul." [34]

When French and British commentators turned to assess the merits of their own colonial regimes, however, both tended to find them largely in the humane and pragmatic good sense of the administrators, and particularly of the *broussards*, the District Commissioners or *commandants de cercle*. Robert Delavignette, an experienced adminis-

[32] F. D. Lugard, *The Dual Mandate in British Tropical Africa*, 2nd Ed. (Edinburgh, 1929), p. 203, quoting the Political Memoranda.

[33] Cf. *The Diaries of Lord Lugard*, Margery Perham and Mary Bull (eds.), Vol. IV (London, 1963), pp. 107, 369, 415, with Louis Sonolet, *L'Afrique Occidentale française* (Paris, 1912), p. 18.

[34] Dr. Barot, *Guide Pratique de l'Européen dans l'Afrique Occidentale à l'usage des militaires, fonctionnaires, commerçants, colons et touristes* (Paris, 1902), pp. 328-31. This interesting work has a commendatory preface by Binger, then Director of African affairs in the Ministry of Colonies.

trator who became director of the national training school for colonial administrators, expounds this doctrine very eloquently. The *commandant*, he writes with reminiscent nostalgia,

> was not a specialist in any branch of administration nor was he lost in an academic theory of administration in general. He was the Chief of a clearly defined country called Damaragam, and Chief in everything that concerned that country. . . . Himself at grips with people and regulations, he had his own rules. He was never taken in by official impostures. . . . He didn't trust ideas from headquarters, whether headquarters was Zinder, Dakar, or Paris.[35]

Delavignette cites approvingly a commandant who "stuck departmental circulars in his trouser pockets before he had read them" and at the end of the day threw trousers and circulars, soaked with the sweat of honest toil, into the laundry basket; the practical experience of such a man was presumed to be a better guide to action than the "cut-and-dried solutions" of the unread circulars (which Delavignette himself would be drafting in the later stages of his career).[35]

A less favorable way of stating this position is to say that this omnicompetent commandant, who "levies taxes, administers justice, polices the country, runs the prisons, directs all public services" was an autocrat whose power was subject to only few and distant checks.[36] Clearly much depended on the personal qualities of the men who exercised such powers. Before World War I, more than half the French administrators were recruited locally, and the service thus included men of very diverse backgrounds, many of whom may have sought service in Africa to escape from aspects of life in Republican France which they found distasteful. Geoffrey Gorer, an angry young traveller of the 1930s, recorded many examples of brutal tyranny, and found the majority of administrators coarse, ignorant, arrogant, and authoritarian; they "were not bourgeois turned *gentilhomme*; they were petits bourgeois turned Caesars." [37] Some of the younger recruits, however, seemed better fitted for African service. After 1920 recruitment was channelled through the Ecole Coloniale in Paris, and some-

[35] Robert Delavignette, *Freedom and Authority in French West Africa* (London, 1950), pp. 6-8, 14.

[36] Suret-Canale, *op. cit.*, II, 95.

[37] Geoffrey Gorer, *Africa Dances* (London, 1935; Penguin Edition, 1945), pp. 63-85. Gorer was later to extend his amateur anthropological observations to the U.S.A.

thing of a hereditary service tradition began to be established during the 1930s. The extension of secondary education in France tended to broaden the social base of recruitment and liberalize the opinions of recruits.[38] A study of the French colonial service being made by Mr. W. B. Cohen should enlarge our understanding of the range of human qualities to be found among French administrators, and of the development of such ideals of the good society as may have guided their service in its work.

Conclusion

It is still perhaps premature to attempt a ripe historical judgment upon any of the European colonial empires; preconceptions arising from connection or national origin rightly and inevitably affect the picture, African perspectives are bound to differ from those of Europeans or Americans. In the foreground of the picture the colonial government and its agents must inevitably bulk large: a bureaucratic machine, which grows to function according to its own rules and assumptions, subject to imperfect control by the representatives of French democracy and still more imperfectly accessible to the complaints of its subjects. The responsibility to the ruled is defined by the rulers themselves: despite the French claim to be freer than the British from racial prejudice, most channels of normal human contact between the two species of *homo sapiens*—"natives" and "Europeans" —seem to have broken down in their empire also. Viewing their rule as a whole, it seems difficult to say who controlled the over-all course of development, and whether the perspiring journeymen who worked the machine had any clear goal in view beyond, at best, responsibly discharging the daily round of paternal duties.

The author's belief, is that, under the Third Republic, French policy was nevertheless influenced, sometimes very remotely, by commitment to some concept of human equality. Applied to peoples of such different cultural background, and at such different stages of social development, as those of French West Africa, this concept often seems to have had little relation to what actually happened. At the minimum it was represented by the positions of the tiny elite of French citizens—defending their small stake in the rights of citizen-

[38] This section owes much to the advice of Mr. William B. Cohen of Stanford University who is studying the recruitment and opinions of French colonial administrators, 1887-1960. See also Delavignette, *Freedom and Authority*, p. 24.

ship, making the most of their educational opportunities, utilizing the French language (and the cultural and political traditions to which it gave access) to develop their own images of the good society as it might exist in West Africa. But these images would seem to have validity, not merely for particular groups, but for Africa as a whole. Specious claims are sometimes made for the benefits of the unity which the French empire brought to West Africa, for it was embodied almost wholly in alien and unrepresentative institutions; but it nevertheless provided conditions for the formulation of wider African consciousness. Even a common prison can be a forcing house for national feeling.

NINE

THE AFRICAN PRESENCE

At the beginning of World War II, French West Africa seemed cast for a traditionally subordinate role; 80,000 African troops were sent to reinforce the French army in Europe. They did not prevent the military catastrophe of June 1940, which brought down the Republic that had shaped the institutions of France's African empire. These great upheavals in Europe opened the way for eventual developments in Africa which French policy had never consciously envisaged: the emergence of independent African states.

The immediate effects were very different. The Government-General, supported more or less readily by most of the Frenchmen in West Africa, accepted the authority of the Vichy regime and repelled the Franco-British naval force which General de Gaulle led to Dakar in September 1940. The following years (still very imperfectly known to historians) saw increasingly authoritarian rule—in part reflecting the ideological outlook of Vichy, in part the direct and indirect demands which wartime conditions made on a hard-pressed administration. Free French officers, operating across the borders of neighboring British territories, won some localized African support; a resistance group in the Senegalese communes, for example, was assisted from Bathurst. A few Africans detected in such activities were summarily shot; the great majority remained indifferent to this European quarrel. Those who resisted the government (or escaped across the frontiers) were commonly moved by personal grievances. For the dislocation of foreign commerce, shortages of food and consumer goods, the demobilization of soldiers, depletion of administrative establishments, all created problems which governments tackled with arbitrary measures. Forced labor was used on an increasing scale: and not only under Vichy. Measures employed after the collapse of Vichy authority in 1943 to raise troops, laborers, or porters, and to extract raw materials for the Allied war effort, were no less harsh in their effects because imposed in a more respectable cause.[1]

Meanwhile, as Allied leaders proclaimed their commitment to create a juster world order after the war, the French provisional government in Algiers was planning the reconstruction of the empire. An influential adviser was Félix Eboué, a Guyanese of African descent, who as Governor of Chad in 1940 had been largely responsible for rallying Equatorial Africa to de Gaulle's Free French movement. Eboué accepted much of the colonial doctrine of the service which he had embellished, while going further than many of his colleagues in seeking to identify and reinvigorate traditional institutions. "The chief," he declared in 1941, "is not an official, he is an aristocrat."[2] These attitudes, reinforced by his wartime contacts with the Nigerian administration, Eboué pressed on an important conference of African administrators and French politicians which met at Brazzaville in the presence of General de Gaulle in January 1944. This meeting agreed that traditional institutions should be encouraged as a means of promoting vigor and activity in colonial life; the governors had relished the freedom from close metropolitan supervision which wartime conditions necessitated, and recommended administrative and economic decentralization in the French empire. A comprehensive program of economic development and social reforms, including the suppression within five years of existing systems of forced labor, was also sketched out. The goal was not African independence, but more genuine assimilation flexibly interpreted;[3] all idea of colonial autonomy or "the eventual constitution of self-governments" was explicitly excluded. Radical reforms were to be implemented within a framework of colonial doctrine inherited from the past, and by means of increased colonial representation in some new Parliamentary Assembly of the indivisible French empire. The details were to be worked out by a Constituent Assembly in which Europeans and Africans from the colonies would be more strongly represented. African leaders voicing

[1] Richard-Molard, A.O.F., pp. 165-7; Suret-Canale, Afrique Noire, II, 568-95. Crowder, Senegal, 2nd Edition, 1966, Chapter Four.

[2] Circular despatch of Nov. 8, 1941 cited Alexandre, "Problème des Chefferies." On Eboué see Albert Maurice, Félix Eboué: Sa Vie et son Oeuvre, Mémoires, Institut Royal Colonial Belge, XXXVII (Bruxelles, 1954).

[3] Governor Toby: "French colonization is based on assimilation, with an element of autonomy, and some more or less attenuated traces of subordination." La Conférence africaine française, Ministère des Colonies (Paris, 1945), p. 74 —the official report of this conference.

aspirations crystallized by wartime discontents were thus for some years directed towards activity in Paris, and collaboration with French politicians.

Political Activity after World War II

Before the war most of these few Frenchmen who were interested in the political status of Africans were men of the Left. Their own political outlook was assimilationist: they gave priority to the equalization of African rights rather than to the ending of colonial rule itself. From 1943, for example, French Communists serving in Africa formed study groups, without encouraging the emergence of autonomous African Communist parties which might prove ideologically immature; they encouraged Africans to expect emancipation as a consequence of working-class revolutions in industrial Europe, not through any short-term development of African society itself. French Socialists were even more successful in assimilating to their party leading citizens of the four Senegalese communes. Lamine Guèye, the first African Doctor of Laws, joined with European residents to form a Senegalese Socialist party which opposed Blaise Diagne, who after associating himself with the Paris Pan-African Congress of 1919 had disappointed his more highly principled followers by drawing closer to the colonial administration. After 1936 Guèye, encouraged by a Socialist Colonial Minister, merged this party into a Senegalese branch of the French Socialists, which for some years was the principal voice of the Senegalese *originaires*. The assimilationist ideal of the French colonial system was thus accepted even by critics of its implementation.

The changes set in motion in 1944 stimulated political activity over a far wider front; the act of holding elections, writes Mrs. Morgenthau "sychronized political developments in territories where political pressure was unequal." [4] West Africa was to send ten representatives to the Constituent Assemblies of 1945 and 1946, five representing a "first college" of French citizens, five a "second college" of subjects. But outside the towns the bases of African political organization were still weak, formed largely by personal, territorial, or ethnic connections; it was still possible for conservative officials or French

[4] Ruth Schachter-Morgenthau, *Political Parties in French-Speaking West Africa* (Oxford, 1964), p. 29.

settlers to influence elections, not only to the first but also to the second college. Nevertheless the six West Africans elected had genuine titles to speak for their constituents.

It was no doubt inevitable that during the constituent process African interests should become subordinated to political shifts within the French majority. Benefits proposed in the draft constitution of April 1946, subsequently rejected by a referendum in which only French citizens could vote, were modified in the text finally adopted in October, in part because of activity by a colonialist pressure group called *Etats Généraux de la Colonisation française*. Nevertheless the advance on the prewar position was considerable. The African colonies became overseas territories of an "indivisible" Fourth Republic (and Togo an "associated territory"); they elected representatives both to its sovereign legislature, the National Assembly, and (in greater proportion) to a consultative Assembly of the French Union. Elective Assemblies were set up in each territory. Although their powers were limited, comparable to those of *conseils généraux*, and professional Governors continued to represent the authority of the indivisible Republic, the status of overseas territories was declared *susceptible d'évolution*. Electoral laws (not incorporated in the constitution) retained restrictions on voting rights, and for some elections the "two college system"; but the constitution conferred citizenship upon all subjects of the empire, although it deliberately failed to define its terms very clearly.[5]

The ending of "subject" status had a significance greater than might be indicated by the increase in the number of registered electors to about one million. To those still unenfranchised it brought freedom, in theory and to an increasing extent in practice, from those features of colonial rule which were most directly oppressive: the bitterly resented *indigénat*, forced labor, restrictions on the right to form trade unions and publish newspapers. It suggested that serious attempts might at last be made to implement the promises of equality implicit in assimilationist theory. It was such a genuine assimilation that the postwar African leadership at first demanded.

[5] A translation of the relevant articles of the Constitution is in Morgenthau, *op. cit.*, pp. 382-5: for summary and commentary see pp. 41-54; also Kenneth Robinson, *The Public Law of Overseas France since the War* (Oxford, 1950); Louis Rolland and Pierre Lampué, *Précis de Droit des Pays d'Outremer* (Paris, 1949).

Economic Development

Taking assimilation seriously implied some effort to reduce the frightening disparity in economic and social standards between France and francophone Africa. The main agent of this was to be an Investment Fund for Economic and Social Development in overseas territories (FIDES), established (along with similar bodies for other parts of the French empire) under a law of 1946. African territorial governments were to draw up ten-year development plans; FIDES, drawing heavily for finance on the French Treasury, would make grants and low-interest loans to expedite the formation of that social and economic infrastructure which had begun to develop slowly in a less bracing financial climate between the wars. Roads, bridges, and port developments: the railway extension to Wagadugu: airports and power stations: agricultural extension and research schemes: schools and colleges, hospitals and medical centers: all were financed through FIDES. In the 1950s France could claim to be spending a much higher proportion of her national income (about 1.5% annually) on aid to the underdeveloped world than any other state; virtually all of this aid was going to some part or other of her former empire, an increasing proportion to tropical Africa. In West Africa it has been estimated that in 1947-56 France provided about 70% of public capital investment (which totalled something approaching $100,000,000) plus over a third of current civil and military expenditure of her colonial governments.[6]

Although these investments undoubtedly spread the benefits of colonial rule more widely, they produced only limited transformations in African economies. Priority was usually given to social investments such as schools and hospitals, often built to lavish standards whose maintenance imposed heavy charges on local budgets. Increases in agricultural and mineral production were expected to follow improvements in infrastructure, and still to be of a nature to serve French needs. The old concept of a *pacte coloniale*, implying continuing interdependence between France and her colonies, was perpetuated,

---

[6] Elliot J. Berg, "The Economic Basis of Political Choice in French West Africa," *American Political Science Review*, LIV (1960), 394-5. Teresa Hayter, "French Aid to Africa—Its Scope and Achievements," *International Affairs*, XLI (1965), 236-51. Official figures about the work of FIDES are summarized in *French Africa: A Decade of Progress*, a brochure published by the French Embassy Press office (New York, 1958).

though refurbished. To facilitate economic integration within the French Union, the produce of francophone Africa was guaranteed fixed prices in the French market. In the early 1950s, when the general rise in raw material prices after the Korean War changed the terms of international trade in favor of primary producers everywhere, this system may have benefited French consumers; when commodity prices fell again later in the decade African producers undoubtedly profited—so long as they continued to produce the crops which France needed. African states became even more dependent on their traditional staple crops, and on the subsidized prices which they received for them from France.

In other respects too economic developments seemed liable to perpetuate French control. The currency board which linked the value of the African and French francs proved a powerful instrument of supervision over economic policies in the different territories. New mineral workings—of phosphates in Senegal, bauxite and diamonds in Guinea, eventually of rich iron deposits in impoverished Mauritania —brought additional wealth to the favored territories, but also the presence of private foreign investors. In Ivory Coast, with its small but influential nucleus of French planters and businessmen established before the war, the number of resident Europeans rose from 4,900 in 1946 to 12,400 in 1951, and there were warning signs that this country might have achieved its relatively rapid rate of growth at the price of fostering West Africa's first "settler problem." [7] Only in the area around Dakar and Rufisque was there any notable development of manufacturing industry, and although this was supported by thirty million dollars of FIDES investments, most of the industrial plant was controlled by foreign capitalists. Very real advantages were gained by some Africans in these postwar years. But the equalization of economic and social standards which seemed the ultimately necessary corollary of assimilationist policies were almost as remote as ever.

In fact the very successes of French postwar policy produced reactions in African society which soon began to undermine its assumptions. Ivory Coast, for example, achieved its rapid increase in agricultural production not so much through its French planters as through a rapid increase in the number and success of African cocoa and coffee farmers. This began in the 1930s and became spectacular dur-

[7] Immanuel Wallerstein, *The Road to Independence* (The Hague, 1964), pp. 35-6.

ing the latter years of the war; by 1947 Africans were producing 90% of the country's growing exports of these crops. Under the Vichy regime and its successors they conflicted bitterly with the administration over marketing arrangements and prices, the allocation of subsidies, and especially over their right to recruit laborers from the limited supply of migrants from the Mossi area. These grievances led the farmers—vigorous entrepreneurs, drawn from many sections of Ivoirian society—to form a *Syndicat Agricole Africain* in 1944, under the presidency of a wealthy Baoulé canton chief and *médécin africain*, Felix Houphouët-Boigny. It was a natural step from there to support Houphouët in seeking election to the Constituent Assemblies, and then, in forming a nationally based political party, the *Parti Democratique de la Côte d'Ivoire* (PDCI).[8]

In urban areas increased economic activity produced new social groupings which manifested themselves through an increasing variety of voluntary associations, from benefit clubs to alumni organizations. These now included trade unions. Although in earlier years there had been quite well organized "turn-outs" of workers in defense of their living standards—by port workers at Cotonou in 1923, by Senegalese railwaymen in 1925, for example—"associations" for such purposes were forbidden to French subjects until 1937, and then only under restrictive conditions which were not removed until 1946. Because of the slow growth of the wage-earning population, only a small part of the population was affected; but teachers and civil servants, miners and railwaymen, truckdrivers and general laborers, began to organize. They were sometimes assisted by political activists, French or African, notably by members of the Communist study groups; but recent writers have warned aginst the tendency to regard African unions as subordinate activities of politicians rather than as expressions of labor interests.[9] True, unions often clashed with the colonial administration, the chief employer of unionized labor as well as the guardian of public order; true, they often assumed political attitudes, sought political allies, sometimes struck for political purposes. In some countries, espe-

[8] This account follows analysis in Morgenthau, *op. cit.* Chapter Five. See also Wallerstein, Road to Independence: Aristide R. Zolberg, *One-Party Government in the Ivory Coast* (Princeton, 1964), pp. 65-77; Amon d'Aby, *La Côte d'Ivoire*, pp. 110-14.

[9] Elliot J. Berg and Jeffrey Butler, "Trade Unions," in James S. Coleman and Carl G. Rosberg, Jr., *Political Parties and National Integration in Tropical Africa* (Berkeley, 1964).

cially Guinea, political and ideological relations between unions and political leaders became close. Yet the unions grew as increasingly spontaneous expressions of the needs and interests of changing African society, which were not always understood by politicians, or indeed by trade unionists abroad. For French-speaking African unions soon reacted against the assimilationist assumptions and paternalist policies of the French labor federations, Communist, Socialist, or Catholic, which originally fostered their growth. Eventually in 1957, Sekou Touré, formerly Secretary-General of the *Confederation Générale du Travail* in Guinea, sponsored an interterritorial federation of African unions known as the *Union Générale des Travailleurs d'Afrique Noire* (UGTAN) rejecting both the Communist WFTU and the Western ICFTU as failing to meet "the special historical requirements of the struggle for emancipation of colonial peoples." [10] Sekou Touré provides an outstanding example of the political commitment of African unionists to anticolonial policies; in taking this commitment he spoke for a small but autochthonous African labor movement.

The New Intellectual Elite

Possibly the most striking example of progressive colonial policies begetting a strong anticolonial reaction is provided by the postwar expansion of opportunities for higher education. The French, even more concerned than the British that standards at the peak of the educational system should be as high as those in France, proceeded very cautiously toward the creation of University institutions in Africa; prewar establishments for higher education were in 1950 grouped into the Institute of Higher Studies at Dakar, which became the eighteenth University of France in 1957 and a fully Senegalese University only in 1964. To train Africans for the highest position it was therefore necessary to provide scholarships liberally for University study in France, thus reverting to the practice long favored by Senegalese citizens, though deplored by many prewar administrators. By 1954, 512 West African students held scholarships for higher studies in France, and perhaps as many were privately financed.[11]

[10] Georges Fischer, "Trade Unions and Decolonisation," *Présence Africaine*, Nos. 34-35 (1961), 144-47.

[11] Roger Bastide, "African Students in France," *International Social Sciences Bulletin*, VIII (1956), 489.

As often happens, study abroad provided nurseries of radical nationalism. The themes of *négritude*, first heard in the 1930s, were now taken up by a larger choir and sung to a widening audience. In November 1947 a cultural review of the Negro world was launched in Paris under the name *Présence Africaine*; it aimed "to help define Negro originality and to hasten its introduction into the modern world." Among its sponsors were Césaire and Senghor (both new Deputies), the American Negro author Richard Wright, and three great French writers, Gide, Camus, and Sartre (who next year contributed a remarkable foreword, *Orphée Noire*, to Senghor's anthology of modern African poetry.) It was argued that by giving priority to asserting their cultural autonomy, francophone Africans were rejecting Nkrumah's advice to seek first the political kingdom. But none of them understood "culture" in any apolitical sense. The director of the new review, Alioune Diop, was a Senegalese member of the *Conseil de la Republique*; its name was a rejoinder to the *présence française* then being defended by colonialists in the Maghreb. In 1956 the journal's supporters undertook their first major common enterprise with English-speaking Africans and Afro-Americans, an International Congress of Negro Writers and Artists at the Sorbonne. A second meeting of this "cultural Bandoeng" was held in Rome in 1959. At these gatherings the link between *négritude* and social or political radicalism, already clearly enough established in many African minds, became quite explicit. "Culture is becoming a formidable means of political action," wrote Alioune Diop in presenting the proceedings of the first Congress; Frantz Fanon, a West Indian psychiatrist who would later be prominent in the war of Algerian independence, roundly asserted that "a colonial country is a racialist country," and saw in cultural renewal a way to produce the will to struggle for "the total liberation of the national territory." [12] At Rome the political implications of the movement became clearer still; learned papers on "The Tonal Structure of Yoruba Poetry" now gave way to addresses on the cultural role of political leadership by President Sekou Touré and Dr. Eric Williams of Trinidad. This expatriate radicalism pro-

[12] *Présence Africaine*, Nos. 8-10 (1956), pp. 5, 128-31. For the Rome congress, Nos. 24-25, 1959. See also Alioune Diop, "The Spirit of Présence Africaine" *Proceedings, First International Congress of Africanists* (London, 1964), pp. 46-51.

foundly influenced the student generations who returned intransigent to Africa in the 1950s and 1960s, determined not to accept assimilationist goals for their country or inferior status for themselves.

Largely through their agency, ideologies crystallized in the cosmopolitan atmosphere of France were fed into the changing societies of West Africa. The demand of these new intellectuals was in the first place that ideas and techniques which they believed to be universally applicable should be used for the emancipation and modernization of their countries. Yet at the same time they sought to anchor these ideas within the traditions and history of those countries. Resistance heroes of the nineteenth century came to be honored by men with whom they had little in common save opposition to French rule. In 1915, a clandestine Dahomean journal had been entitled *Le Recadaire* [traditional Royal messenger] *de Behanzin*; an Afro-Parisian restaurant of the 1950s was called *Le Samori*. More important, new political leaders in the different territories began to build up connections among groups prominent in traditional society—chiefs, *marabouts*, Harrisite churches, leaders of country societies like the Poro, *dyulas*, with their important networks of interterritorial relationships —as well as among leaders of more modern associations. Gradually demands for progress and equality became demands for greater political independence.

International Pressures

Pressures in the direction of political independence also came because of changes in international power politics. After the war the pace of decolonization was at first set in Asia, where Japanese victories had demolished many of the myths on which European empires depended for survival. In Indo-China it quickly became plain that the prospects offered by the French Union (as interpreted by French policy-makers) would not satisfy Asian aspirations. In December 1946 a fierce civil war began, which was to have far-reaching implications for all five continents. The independence of British India, achieved somewhat more peacefully in 1947, also raised doubts about the future of colonial empires, even if reconstructed. The development of the "cold war" made Soviet Russia anxious to exploit, the United States to eliminate, the "contradictions" inherent in the colonial situation.

Already in the last stages of the war it had become clear that such contradictions existed in French North Africa.[13] Now the nationalists of Tunisia and Morocco sought support against reactionary colonists and authoritarian administrators in quarters which were potentially interested in West Africa also. The Tunisian and Moroccan questions were debated by the United Nations General Assembly in December 1952, despite French opposition. Article 73 of the U.N. Charter, which in its English text prescribes an obligation "to develop self-government" in dependent territories, in its French version required colonial powers only to "développer leur capacité de s'administrer elles-mêmes"; in practice it was becoming clear that world opinion expected France to act according to the Anglo-Saxon version.[14] North African leaders also sought support in Cairo, center not only of the Arab League but of the modernizing trends in Islamic thought associated with the renascent University of al Azhar. Although West African *marabouts* still generally represented older, less intellectual, forms of Islam, political and social ideas from the Middle East were now influencing Africans of Muslim origin who had been educated in secular colonial schools. The outbreak of war in Algeria in November 1954 strengthened both the political and religious pressures which were making many articulate West Africans reconsider their relations with the French Union, although their Deputies in Paris for several years tended to acquiesce in French attempts at repression, and even their employment of African troops.[15] Tunisian and Moroccan independence, achieved in 1956, also had effects south of the Sahara.

There were other changes even nearer home. In 1950, Nkrumah's success in creating a broadly based nationalist party in the Gold Coast produced a great acceleration in the timing of political change in all British West African territories. This raised special problems in the French Trust territory of Togoland. The most politically conscious Togolese were the Ewe people of the south of whom there were, officially, 174,000 under French rule (certainly a deliberate understatement), 137,000 in the British Trust territory, and 376,000 in the Gold Coast. After the war Ewe leaders began to petition the U.N. for unification of their country under British tutelage, thereby

---

[13] See the volumes in this series by John C. Cairns on *France* (1965) and by Richard M. Brace, on *Morocco: Algeria: Tunisia* (1964).

[14] Rene Massigli, "New Conceptions of French Policy in Tropical Africa," *International Affairs*, XXXIII (1957), 407-8.

[15] Morgenthau, *op. cit.*, p. 82.

reactivating French suspicions of British imperialist intrigues. In 1952, with an independent Ghana now imminently possible, Ewe admirers of Nkrumah began to demand the integration of all British Togoland into Ghana; it was clear that they would next demand the integration of French Togoland also. Other Ewes, led by Sylvanus Olympio, demanded the reunification of the two Togolands first, with federation with Ghana perhaps to follow later. Each program enlisted some support in the United Nations; ultimately in 1956 the people of British Togoland voted by plebiscite for union with Ghana. French administrators, determined to keep their territory within the French Union, supported Grunitsky's *Parti Togolaise du Progrès*, which was prepared to advocate such a course if based on rapid reforms within the territory itself. In 1955 the Togolese territorial assembly voted unanimously in favor of the early liquidation of French trusteeship; plans were hurriedly made to turn Togo into an autonomous republic within the French Union before the possibly embarrassing arrival of a Ghanaian representative at the United Nations.[16]

If little Togoland achieved internal self-government it would be difficult to resist comparable reforms in A.O.F. By 1955 it was becoming more apparent that African aspirations could not be satisfied within a unitary Republic. The new organs of the French Union had shown little vitality; the French National Assembly, where effective power still lay, remained preoccupied with domestic and European affairs, or with those overseas territories which threatened open revolt. It was true that, as the coalition which provided the immediately postwar governments with their majorities dissolved into ever smaller and more deeply divided political factions, groups of overseas Deputies could wield more political influence than some Frenchmen had expected. "It's the Madagascans who are making the law!" cried one disgruntled Deputy after a particularly close vote. By allying with French parties and concentrating on concrete local issues African Deputies were able both to influence some administrative policies and to secure amendments to the electoral law, important extensions of the franchise, improved labor legislation and, eventually, reforms in local government.[17] It is misleading to speak of the postwar decade as

[16] James S. Coleman, *Togoland*, International Conciliation, No. 509 (New York, 1956); Robert Cornevin, *Histoire du Togo* (Paris, 1959), pp. 381-98.
[17] Kenneth Robinson, "Local Government Reform in French Tropical Africa," *Journal of African Administration*, VIII (1956).

a period of *immobilisme;* the colonies were making quite rapid progress along the road indicated to them in 1946. But gradually some political leaders began to look toward a different road altogether.

The Road toward Independence

The first attempt to unify movements of African protest from the various colonies was made in October 1946, when a number of political leaders and Deputies met at Bamako to found an interterritorial party, the *Rassemblement Democratique Africain* or R.D.A., dedicated to the emancipation (not the political independence) of Africans. But the Senegalese leaders Guèye and Senghor, and some from other territories, were deterred from participating by their French Socialist allies, one of whom was Colonial Minister. The only French party represented at Bamako was the Communists; until 1950 they maintained a tactical alliance with the R.D.A. deputies in Paris, and their doctrinal influence, established by the study groups, remained strong. It is however important to understand that African leaders did not oppose French policies because they had been indoctrinated by Communists, but because many of these policies pressed hard upon their people.

The leader of the R.D.A. was Houphouët-Boigny, whose standing with the Ivoirian public was enormously strengthened by his part in the French parliamentary debates of 1946 on the abolition of the detested *indigénat* and the systems of forced labor which it sanctioned. At first he believed that the alliance of the strong French Communist party offered the best tactical method of resisting hostile administrators and settlers, and of securing further reform within the assimilationist framework of the French Community. In 1949-50 Houphouët's own supporters in the Ivory Coast were the target for determined attempts at repressions by Governor Péchoux, and substantial numbers of Ivoirians were killed, wounded, jailed, or victimized.[18] In these trials the alliance of French Communists proved more of an embarrassment than an asset, providing an internationally acceptable justification for the repressive policy which *colons* and others favored. Moreover, Houphouët began to realize that Communists might show the same reservations as other Frenchmen in putting assimilation into whole-hearted effect; had they not retained office in the French government which repressed the Malagasy revolt

[18] Morgenthau, *op cit.,* pp. 188-202.

of 1947? After internal debate, the R.D.A. broke with the Communist alliance in 1950. By claiming greater independence of action it was, perhaps unconsciously, taking a first step toward a policy envisaging national independence for African states.[19]

Many of the African leaders who remained outside the R.D.A. remained allied to the Socialists (who participated in French governments up to 1951 and again from 1956 until 1958). Some of these represented the so-called "patron parties," which depended largely on the support of chiefs or ethnic representatives, and on the direct or indirect favor of the colonial administration. The Sudanese Progressive Party, for example, drew much of its support from former subjects of the Tokolor empire, for whom the French occupation had brought relief from some burdens at least. The Socialists in Senegal, who dominated politics immediately after the war, were based among those *originaires* of the four communes who had so long accepted assimilationist goals. The newly enfranchised citizens of the interior found these less comprehensible, even though Senghor, that living testimonial that assimilation could work, could be readily acclaimed as their spokesman. But Senghor himself, disappointed with the pace of postwar reforms, was now reacting against political as well as cultural assimilation. In 1948 he founded a new party, the *Bloc Démocratique Sénégalais*, based primarily on the new rural voters. The Socialists, it is true, maintained a strong base in the countryside until 1951 by their alliance with the *grands marabouts* of the conservative Muridiyya, but the B.D.S. was supported by influential leaders of the rival Tijaniyya. The political history of Senegal henceforth centers upon the extension and consolidation of this party, under a succession of different names. Organizationally the story is complex, full of splits, feuds and mergers; but its theme is the construction of an ever-stronger connection of "clans"—ethnic, religious, or personal-interest groups capable of influencing the expanding electorate—until (with the absorption in June 1966 of the dissident intellectuals of the *Parti de Regroupement Africain*) Senghor's party could claim fairly comprehensive control of power at the grass roots. Doctrinally socialism remained part of Senghor's ideology; but by

[19] Michael Crowder, "Independence as a Goal in French West African Politics," pp. 25-7 in William H. Lewis (ed.), *French-Speaking Africa: the Search for Identity* (New York, 1965). It is worth noting that, after the crisis of 1949-50, race relations seem to have improved very greatly in the Ivory Coast. There as elsewhere, Europeans have held office in African governments and parties.

1960 he and his contemporaries were increasingly seeking to identify a distinctively "African socialism," which by cherishing the intellectual, spiritual, and sociological inheritance of Africa would avoid the rigidity of European theorists, and find means of escaping the miseries which in Europe had attended the preliminary period of capital formation.[20] Politically the new party, like the R.D.A. elsewhere, moved toward demanding some form of African independence.

Both hoped to combine independence with the continued unity of A.O.F. This unity had very wide support during the fifties among articulate Africans. The *dyulas*, one of the groups in West African society which had always been somewhat cosmopolitan in their interests and outlook, played a considerable role in building up the R.D.A. especially in the Ivory Coast and Mali, but also at the interterritorial level. Among the educated class too there was much pan-West-African feeling. Studies in Paris or at Ponty, as is often pointed out, drew together an elite from all A.O.F. In the federal public service its members continued to mingle in pursuit of common purposes, and in French, unlike British, territories, public servants played prominent roles in politics. The "slate" of African candidates put forward in 1945 for the *commune mixte* of Abijan included six Senegalese, two Guineans, two Dahomeans, and only eight Ivoirians, and there were many more examples of men born in one territory achieving political eminence in another.[21] However, the failure in 1946 to provide representative institutions for the federation partially checked this tendency. Within the territorial structure of politics, jealousy of "strangers" tended to develop among peoples who had enjoyed fewer privileges than the old Senegalese "citizens," fewer educational opportunities than Dahomean Catholics. Even the National Assembly in Paris, while providing opportunities for territorial representatives to cooperate in African interests, frequently saw them divided for reasons of political tactics.[22] So the growing aspiration for independence in unity was not represented by a unified independence movement.

Even after the French elections of 1956, which seemed to improve

[20] Léopold Sédar Senghor, *Nation et Voie africaine du Socialisme* (Paris, 1961) (English translation by Mercer Cook, N.Y., 1964). See also William H. Friedland and Carl G. Rosberg, Jr. (eds.), *African Socialism* (Stanford, 1964).

[21] F. J. Amon d'Aby, *op. cit.*, pp. 46-50; Morgenthau, *op. cit.*, pp. 10-22.

[22] Morgenthau, *op. cit.*, p. 124.

the bargaining power of the African Deputies, the initiative still lay with France. Internal and external pressures alike indicated that radical constitutional reforms were needed; but it seemed possible to recognize African identity without sacrificing the concept of a French Union. Free elections were miraculously returning accredited African spokesmen prepared to see whether independence could be reconciled with some new concept of *la République une et divisible*. Some Frenchmen however hoped to maintain the unity by multiplying divisions. The *loi-cadre* of June 1956, sponsored by the Socialist Ministers Defferre and Mollet, while establishing universal suffrage on a common roll in all French overseas territories, opened the way for further constitutional development in each of them along the lines already envisaged for Togo. A series of statutory instruments provided for each territorial assembly to elect a council of government, whose members would enjoy ministerial status and a measure of control over certain local services, subject to the continuing authority of the governor in many important respects. Control of military and foreign policy, and to a considerable extent of finance and justice, was still vested in the metropolitan government. African representation in Paris was again increased both in the National Assembly and in the executive. Houphouët-Boigny was given prominent office in each French cabinet between 1956 and 1959.[23]

Other African leaders suspected that this policy of devolution within an essentially unitary empire was designed to "Balkanize" Africa, and perpetuate French control. Senghor and Sekou Touré both regretted the absence of representative institutions for A.O.F. as a whole; indeed, the functions of the existing Grand Council were reduced. In September 1957 the R.D.A. Congress at Bamako, while expressing genuine interest in continued free association with France, urged the establishment of a democratic federal executive; meanwhile Senghor and other party leaders moved decidedly in the same direction.[24] The condition of "true interdependence" among the peoples of the French Union seemed to be constitutional recognition of the unity of West (and similarly of Equatorial) Africa. Nevertheless, African leaders now had to perform on the stages provided

---

[23] Kenneth Robinson, "Constitutional Reform in French Tropical Africa," *Political Studies*, VI (1958), 45-69; Morgenthau, *op. cit.*, pp. 65-73.
[24] André Blanchet, *L'Itinéraire des partis africains depuis Bamako* (Paris, 1958); Crowder, *op. cit.*, pp. 28-32.

for them—the councils of ministers and assemblies of the respective territories. As they assumed responsibility in these spheres, they inevitably found the concrete local interests of their own countries weighing heavily against the more general claims of pan-Africanism.

One leader, Houphouët-Boigny, was indeed becoming increasingly attached to the new formula, of small autonomous states entering into direct relations with the French Union. This was not merely because he enjoyed the prestigious role which he personally was called upon to play in French politics, and distrusted the idea of total independence, the savor of which had clearly been wafted from Ghana to the Bamako congress. The Ivory Coast was now much the richest territory in French West Africa; only Senegal had a comparable national income. A powerful federal government would collect over a third of its revenue from Ivoirians, who would derive less direct benefit then the Senegalese from its expenditure.[25] Against the growing "federalist" opinion, Houphouët remained a strong territorialist: faced by mounting enthusiasm for independence he (like Senghor) wished to retain organic links with France. Under the Fifth Republic a solution emerged which nobody had wanted; nine small independent West African states.

De Gaulle, carried to power by the Fourth Republic's failure to solve the Algerian problem, still hoped by equalizing the rights of citizens to preserve France's connection with the African territories; but he was determined not to risk new colonial wars in order to do so. French opinion, never so emotionally involved with the tropical colonies as with the Maghreb, was beginning to doubt whether they were worth the cost of economic aid and preferential trade policies; a disenchanted journalist's articles in *Paris-Match* in 1956 produced a name, *Cartierisme*, for this fashionable attitude. The draft constitution of the Fifth Republic offered the overseas territories complete internal self-government under a Prime Minister, together with full rights of citizenship in the Community, which was now to replace the French Union. The Executive Council of the Community, with a French majority of one, would continue to control foreign affairs, defense and major aspects of economic and financial policy. Any member state could, however, determine to leave the Community; and during the preparations for the referendum on the new constitution de Gaulle agreed, with very bad grace, that a negative vote by

[25] Berg, *op. cit.*, pp. 401-4.

any territory would constitute such a rejection of autonomy within the Community in favor of full independence—with presumably dire consequences attached, including the risk of losing French economic aid.

African political leaders had now to consider whether to advise their supporters to accept Balkanized autonomy within a Community whose future evolution could not be clearly foreseen, or to vote on principle for an independence which would also imply Balkanization, at least until the new states re-established unity among themselves. Most leaders hesitated, but only two finally called their followers to reject the constitution. One was Djibo Bakary of Niger, who was however unable to secure more than 21% of the votes, in face of strong pressure from French administrators and troops upon the widely dispersed electorate. The other was Sekou Touré, whose position in Guinea was far stronger. Working out of his base in a trade union movement much strengthened by mining developments, he had built the *Parti Democratique de Guinée* into a strong and nation-wide party, uniting trade unionists and countrymen against organizations which tended to represent sectional ethnic loyalties, or the influence of chiefs backed by administrators. Already in December 1957 P.D.G. ministers had eliminated the unrepresentative canton chiefs from local administration, substituting a framework of elected local councils through which the party's own influence was enabled to spread. Sekou Touré, a militant anti-imperialist of Marxist background, was the hero of radical students and Trade Unionists from all A.O.F., who looked to him for a stand on radical principle. In de Gaulle's own presence Sekou Touré therefore affirmed that poverty in freedom was preferable to riches in slavery; when he called for a negative vote in the referendum 97% of the voters complied, even though the voting was largely under the auspices of French administrators.

Guinea had chosen independence against French wishes; the consequences were a sudden wholesale withdrawal of French personnel and financial support; a search for alternative sources of aid, involving troubled, though periodically close, relations with Communist powers; and in foreign relations a reputation as the sea-green incorruptible enemy of imperialism, which Guinean leaders have consistently sought to preserve. Over the next three years the remaining overseas territories, with French acquiescence, took less stormy roads to independence. In both Sudan and Senegal political leaders began to promote the formation of a federation, under the prestigious name of Mali, which would enjoy full independence with a reorganized and closely-knit community. Houphouët-Boigny, still opposed to federalism but unable wholly to discount the popular appeal of the idea of unity, persuaded the governing parties of Niger (where Djibo Bakary had now been ousted), Dahomey, and Upper Volta to join Ivory Coast in a much looser confederation, the *Conseil de l'Entente*.[26]

What was to be the international status of these two rival groupings? When the Sudanese and Senegalese began to negotiate successfully with de Gaulle for the independence of Mali, Houphouët, to save his prestige, and his thesis that fraternal cooperation with France would prove more fruitful than militancy, suddenly requested and secured immediate independence for the four members of the *Entente*. In the same month, August 1960, the Mali federation broke apart; differences of interest, ideology, and personal outlook between Senegalese and Sudanese, which might have become blurred within a multilateral federation, proved too sharp to permit their monogamous marriage. Former Sudan inherited the name of Mali, and Senegal entered the United Nations in its own right. When Mauritania, which because of her northern connections had remained aside from these groupings, became independent in November 1960, all nine colonies had confirmed their status as separate republics.[27]

African Unity versus National Identity

How far had they acquired distinctive national identities? To a considerable degree it seemed that these might remain to be shaped by the leaders holding office at the moment of independence. The tendency was now for power, in the provinces as well as the capitals, to become concentrated in a single (not necessarily a sole) party, or sometimes in a coalition of parties. Practical and ideological justification for this could be found by reference to the tremendous problems of national mobilization and growth which faced the new regimes. Political activity by rival parties, it was argued, was essentially divisive; at best it represented a waste of resources and leadership which African countries could ill afford, at worst it might arouse dangerously

---

[26] In 1966 they were joined by Togo, fully independent since April 1960.

[27] For these developments, see Crowder, *op. cit.*, pp. 32-41; William J. Foltz, *From French West Africa to the Mali Federation* (New Haven, 1965); Immanuel Wallerstein, "How Seven States Were Born in French West Africa," *Africa Report*, VI (March 1961).

unrealistic expectations among an unsophisticated electorate, and perhaps revive old sectional antagonisms. Rival parties were in fact unnecessary if the essential democratic processes could take place within a single organization. Marxists had taught that parties represented conflicting class interests, but in Africa "there exists only one and the same class, that of the dispossessed." [28] The important division in the world was between those striving to maintain the inequalities associated with imperialism and those struggling to remove them: between those peoples, largely white in pigmentation, where even manual workers enjoyed full stomachs and social services, and those whom Fanon called, in the title of a powerful and increasingly influential political tract, *Les Damnés de la Terre*.[29] Whether the struggle of the new nations was believed to be against privileged classes, exploiting races, or simply against harsh historical conditions which they had inherited, it seemed plausible to argue that it could best be waged by a united party. A few African leaders (mostly anglophone) challenged this thesis with the traditional arguments of liberal democracy, but in the early years of independence they seemed to be fighting a losing cause.

Although all new states moved towards single-party systems, these were of differing character. Historical conditions in the various territories largely determined what qualities were needed for effective political leadership. Senegal, with its longer experience of an assimilationist tradition, remained somewhat more permissive than Guinea towards political opposition; the Ivory Coast, with its enterprising small capitalists, was less eager to establish state control over the economy. The Republic of Dahomey, whose three distinct historical regions each produced their own party organizations, saw repeated attempts to achieve a lasting balance among them by coalitions or mergers. In this confused situation the educated elite of the coastal areas, with its cosmopolitan outlook and its high expectations of employment, proved more skillful in drafting political programs than in finding a basis for developing the economy; by the mid-1960s many Dahomeans were looking to the army rather than politicians for national leadership. Yet whatever political system emerged would

[28] Sekou Touré, quoted Immanuel Wallerstein, "The Political Ideology of the P.D.G.," *Présence Africaine*, No. 40 (1962), p. 31; of Madeira Keita, "Le Parti Unique en Afrique," *Présence Africaine*, No. 30 (1960), pp. 29-54.
[29] Frantz Fanon, *Les Damnés de la Terre*, Paris, 1961: English edition, *The Wretched of the Earth* (London, 1965).

surely find a role for the articulate intellectuals of this "West African Latin Quarter." They, as well as the traditional representatives of Bariba, Fon and Gun, were part of Dahomey's inheritance from history.

Even where it might seem, as in Mali, that the new leadership had been shaped by radical ideologies from overseas the inheritance of national history remained extremely strong. Leaders of the governing party attributed their emphasis on social egalitarianism to the responsibility of Muslims to care for the poor and weak, not merely to the Marxism which had certainly influenced the formation of their policy. The almost puritanical intransigence of their principles in questions of internal social discipline and international anticolonial solidarity reflected in part the historical zealotry of the towns of the desert marches, still shaken by the traumatic shock of the violent incursion of Desbordes and Archinard. Malian emphasis on collective decisions by the leaders of the party, and on broad popular activity at the grass roots, represented a conscious concern to reconcile sectional differences, not only ethnic ones but others which might perpetrate the divisions of earlier centuries. The *Union Soudanaise*, originally manned largely by leaders of groups distrusted by the colonial administration, incorporated many who had worked more closely with the French; its Muslim leaders were careful to establish a secular state. The revival of the name of medieval Mali, and the emphasis on President Modibo Keita's descent from its rulers, projected the basis of national unity sufficiently far into the past to allow more recent causes of disunity to be played down. Mali's leaders included men with unusually keen senses of history; even if many were also well versed in foreign ideas and ideologies, it would be a disastrous error to imagine that these were uncritically absorbed by political innocents.[30]

Another political movement which discovered a basis for national identity in historical experience was the Mauritanian People's Party of President Mokhtar Ould Daddah (the first Mauritanian to graduate from a western university). At first Mokhtar's followers resembled a typical patron party, based upon traditional elites and subservient to the French administration; they held aloof from the R.D.A. on grounds of Mauritania's cultural affinity with the Maghreb,

[30] Morgenthau, *Political Parties*, Chap. VII; also her chapter, with Thomas Hodgkin, on "Mali" in Coleman and Rosberg, *op. cit.*

yet resisted Morocco's claim for union. After 1961 Mokhtar, fortified by revenue from newly developed mines, worked to form a broadly based party capable not only of modernizing the life of the desert nomads but of playing a role in international politics as mediator between tropical Africa and the Maghreb. The Islamic character of the state and its promotion of the Arabic language created problems among the Negro minority in the south; but it may be that this revival of the historic role of the desert peoples as the link between Muslims north and south of the Sahara will provide the clue to Mauritania's national identity in the modern world.[31]

The Outlook

What, finally, can be said about the future prospects of these nine states? Their economies continue to manifest the syndrome of under-development, with variable signs of improvement. Growth has been limited and localized; national incomes still depend heavily on a few primary products, for which world prices in recent years have been tending to fall. Africans are still caught up in what René Dumont calls "the vicious circle of an underproductive agriculture, carried out by undernourished men on unfertilized soil." [32] Continuing access to supplies of foreign capital seems essential if there is to be any hope of increasing the pace of development.

In some respects, France may seem more strongly committed than other ex-colonial states to providing this. The powers of supervision which she maintained over the currency, and so indirectly over the economy, of members of the franc zone were to some extent preserved when in 1959 the Currency Board was transformed into a Central Bank with close links with the French Treasury. (But Guinea left the franc zone and Mali has loosened her ties with it.) These arrangements meant that the African states retained special customs relationships and other economic links, as a sort of free trade area; they have subsequently joined in a varied pattern of international organizations and *ad hoc* associations, such as that through which Senegal, Mali, Mauritania, and Guinea plan to develop the resources of the Senegal river. Although some of these bodies extend beyond

    [31] Clement H. Moore, "One-Partyism in Mauritania," *JMAS*, III (1965), 409-20.
    [32] René Dumont, *L'Afrique Noire est Mal Partie* (Paris, 1962), p. 18. English edition, *False Start in Africa* (London, 1966).

the francophone area, most former French colonies remain heavily dependent for development funds on FAC—the *Fonds d'Aide et Co-opération* which in 1959 replaced FIDES; and still look in large degrees to France for civil servants and technical assistance. But not all Frenchmen recognize a responsibility to continue the supply; the effective collapse of the Community concept strengthened the tendency towards *cartierisme*. In 1964 the Jeanneney Report proposed some redeployment of French foreign aid, including a reduction in the proportion allotted to tropical Africa and the elimination of direct subsidies to recurrent government expenditure; only the Dahomean budget was still so subsidized in 1965.[33]

The effects on France's former colonies of her membership in the European Economic Community may also be far-reaching. Some Africans suspect this organization of "neocolonialist" purposes. France has agreed to abandon by 1967 the preferential prices for primary products which at present boost the value of African exports; but in return the African Associates of the E.E.C. (including all our nine states except Guinea) can hope to obtain access to a European market of 170,000,000 people, probably on terms guaranteeing some stability of prices. They may also hope to find new sources of capital in the European Investment Bank and the Community's Development Fund. The Yaoundé Convention of Association (1963) also expressed an intention to "further the industrialization of the associated states and the diversification of their economies." [34] If the E.E.C. takes this responsibility seriously, the charge of neocolonialism will sound unconvincing.

It is not merely the economic prospects however which make friends of Africa apprehensive. In analyzing the social malaise of the new nations the French agronomist Dumont and the revolutionary Fanon find much common ground. The first fruits of decolonization seem to have gone to a small "national bourgeoisie" of officials and intellectuals, remote from economic reality in their enjoyment of privileges secured under colonial rule. Unlike a classical bourgeoisie these men are rarely interested in productive enterprise, even for profit; government employment, the principal industry, is sufficient

[33] Hayter, *op. cit.*, pp. 243-44.
[34] Tom Soper, "The EEC and Aid to Africa," *International Affairs*, XLI (1965), 475. See also Thomas Balogh, "Africa and the Common Market." *Journal of Common Market Studies*, I (1962), 79-112.

as an end in itself. In the name of racial equality African officials
have fought to be paid the same as foreigners with comparable training and responsibilities; that they should be discriminated against
in their own country does indeed seem scandalous. But no less a
scandal—in fact a potentially still more explosive one—is revealed
when the standard of living of this African elite is compared with
that of their kinsmen who still work with their hands. Increased exports achieved by African farmers and miners are balanced by increased imports of consumption goods, official limousines, and spirits,
so that this "new class" may enjoy the standards of high living which
their colonial rulers taught them to emulate. In the new African perspective practices which Europe finds wholly acceptable and func-
tional may look different. European workers struggled for the payment
of Members of Parliament, so that poor men might be enabled to
enter the legislature; African Deputies, paid at comparable rates for
shorter sessions, need to be exceptionally strongminded if their salaries
are not to form a barrier between themselves and their constituents.
The "Balkanization" of 1956-60 multiplied the opportunities to create
prestigious and well-paid offices and to build presidential palaces in
the spirit of Versailles; Dumont makes telling comparisons with the
court of Louis XVI.[35] By the mid-sixties discontent with this situation
was manifest in many quarters, although revolt was tending to follow
the pattern of 18th Brumaire rather than that of 14th July.

Economically and socially then there were grounds for pessimism
about Africa's "false start"—even more so perhaps in francophone
than in anglophone Africa. It remained uncertain how far the position
might be redeemed by the political leaders, for they were evidently
approaching these problems in very different ways. Each government
was seeking its own balance between the perils of "neocolonialism"
and the necessity of seeking overseas aid. Mali and Guinea, two states
which were making serious endeavors to overcome their shortage of
capital by mobilizing their own resources of labor and energy for
"human investments" had perhaps avoided the more glaring social
inequalities at some risk of creating opposition by authoritarian discipline and uniform austerity. But even Sekou Touré could be accused of compromising with anti-imperialist principles;[36] while on
the other side even Houphouët-Boigny could point, in justification

[35] Dumont, *op. cit.*, pp. 63-71; cf. Fanon, *op. cit.*, pp. 121-63.
[36] B. Ameillon, *La Guinée, Bilan d'une Indépendance* (Paris, 1964).

of manifest dependence on French economic and military assistance, to signs of advance upon the colonial economic situation. Between these two protagonists of opposite approaches, other leaders took up a variety of positions: Mali sought to combine socialist neutralism and association with the E.E.C., Senegal displayed anticolonial zeal in the councils of the Organisation of African Unity while retaining French troops on her own soil. It is beyond the scope of this study to forecast which of these varied political postures will provide the best starting point for attacking the intractable problems which history has bequeathed to these nine African states.

Jacques Richard-Molard, *Afrique Occidentale française* (Paris, 1952), is a stimulating introduction to the region by a geographer of wide interests. A broadly conceived work of Marxist inspiration is Jean Suret-Canale, *Afrique Noire, Occidentale et Centrale: Géographie—Civilisations—Histoire,* Two vols. (Paris, 1958, 1964). Robert Cornevin discusses both traditional and colonial history in his *Histoire du Togo* (Paris, 1959), and *Histoire du Dahomey* (Paris, 1962); and there is a brief survey of *Le Sénégal et la Gambie* by Hubert Deschamps in the series *Que-Sais-je?* (Paris, 1964). A great deal of general information is contained in Virginia Thompson and Richard Adloff, *French West Africa* (London, 1958).

The basic work on the medieval history of the Western Sudan was for long Maurice Delafosse, *Haut-Sénégal-Niger,* Tome II, *L'Histoire* (Paris, 1912); this officially commissioned work by the most scholarly of the early French administrators draws on a great deal of orally transmitted testimony, as well as documentary sources. But it is often difficult to distinguish and evaluate these sources, and many of his conclusions can no longer be upheld. The leading modern authority on this period is Raymond Mauny. Besides his many articles, notably in the publications of the *Institut Français d'Afrique Noire* (IFAN) his *Tableau géographique de l'ouest africain au moyen age* (Dakar, 1961), now provides the essential starting point for work on this period. More popular introductions are provided by E. W. Bovill, *Caravans of the Old Sahara* (London, 1933), republished in revised form as *The Golden Trade of the Moors* (London, 1958); and Basil Davidson, *Lost Cities of Africa* (Boston, 1959).

A valuable but often controversial and over-dogmatic account of the early Muslim empires will be found in J. Spencer Trimingham, *A History of Islam in West Africa* (London, 1962), a sequel to his *Islam in West Africa* (Oxford, 1959). Vincent Monteil, *L'Islam Noir* (Paris, 1964), is a wide ranging survey of past and present. Alphonse Gouilly, *L'Islam dans l'Afrique Occidentale française* (Paris, 1952) draws on older, more specialized works by Paul Marty; he is more interested in recent developments than in history. The fullest work on Mali remains C. Monteil, "Les Empires du Mali," in *BCEHSAOF,* XII (1929); recent commentaries may be found in the special issues of *Notes Africaines* (IFAN, Dakar) for April and June 1959; in N. Levtzion "The Thirteenth and Fourteenth Century Kings of Mali," *JAH*, IV (1963); and in various articles by Tamsir Djibril Niane published in *Recherches Africaines* (Conakry) since 1959. On Songhai, see Jean Rouch, *Contribution à l'histoire des Songhay* (Dakar, 1953), and J. O. Hunwick, "Ahmad Baba and the Moroccan Invasion of the Sudan," *JHSN*, II (1962), pp. 311-28. There is a brief but stimulating contribution from Poland in M. Malowist, "The Social and Economic Stability of the Western Sudan in the Middle Ages," *Past and Present* No. 35 (April, 1966). For one of the most important non-Muslim peoples, consult Charles Monteil, *Les Bambaras du Ségou et du Kaarta* (Paris, 1924) and Louis Tauxier, *Histoire des Bambaras* (Paris, 1942). For some indications of the lines along which modern scholars are revising the history of the whole pre-European period, see *The Historian in Tropical Africa*, Jan Vansina, Raymond Mauny, and L. V. Thomas (eds.) (London, 1964).

Many of the original sources for the history of the medieval period are in need of modern editions. Existing translations include:

El Bekri [Al Bakri], *Description de l'Afrique septentrionale*, trans. de Slane (Alger, 1913).

Voyages d'Ibn Batouta, trans. C. Defrémery and B. R. Sanguinetti, Vol. IV (Paris, 1853-59). The translation for the Hakluyt Society by Sir Hamilton Gibb has not yet reached this volume.

Jean Léon l'Africain, *Description de l'Afrique*, trans. A. Epaulard, two vols. (Paris, 1956). Book VII deals with Sudan. Jon Pory's English translation of 1600 (*The History and Description of Africa and of the Notable Things Therein Contained* by Al-Hassan ibn-Mohammed al-Wezaz al-Fasi) was reprinted in three volumes by the Hakluyt Society in 1896.

Mahmoud Kati, *Tarikh el-Fettach*, trans. O. Houdas and M. Delafosse (Paris, 1913). (Reprinted 1964.)

Abderrahman es-Sadi, *Tarikh es-Soudan*, trans. O. Houdas (Paris, 1900) (Reprinted 1964.)

There is a substantial corpus of evidence available for coastal areas, from the fifteenth century onward, in the writings of European travellers, traders, and compilers. Here too critical editions are badly needed; many of these authors quote extensively without acknowledgment from earlier writers, and many have suffered from bad translators or editors. The following sample list merely indicates some of the material available:

Gomes Eannes de Azurara, *The Chronicle of the Discovery and Conquest of Guinea*, trans. C. R. Beazley and E. Prestage, Hakluyt Society, first series, Vols. 95, 100 (London, 1896, 1899).

The Voyages of Cadamosto and other documents, G. R. Crone, ed., Hakluyt Society, second series, Vol. 80 (London, 1937).

Valentim Fernandes, *Description de la Côte Occidentale d'Afrique*, ed., Theodore Monod, A. Texeira da Monta, Raymond Mauny (Bissau, 1951).

Olfert Dapper, *Description de l'Afrique* (Amsterdam, 1686). Said to be an unreliable translation.

P. Cultru (ed.), *Premier Voyage du Sieur de la Courbe fait à la coste d'Afrique en 1685* (Paris, 1913).

William Bosman, A *New and Accurate Description of the Coast of Guinea* (London, 1705).

John Barbot, A *Description of the Coasts of North and South Guinea*, in Awnsham and John Churchill, A *Collection of Voyages and Travels*, vol. V (London, 1732).

Archibald Dalzel, *The History of Dahomey* (London, 1793). Compiled by men who had resided there, and who were concerned to defend the slave trade against its British critics.

Trimingham's interpretation of the Muslim resurgence of the eighteenth and nineteenth centuries has been criticized by Thomas L. Hodgkin, "Islam, History and Politics," *JMAS*, I (1963), and "Islam and National Movements in West Africa," *JAH*, III (1962); also by H. F. Charles Smith, "The Islamic Revolutions of the Nineteenth Century," *JHSN*, II (1961) and in a savage review in *Ibadan*, No. 15 (1963). A very important collection of traditions has been recorded by Amadou Hampaté Ba and Jean Daget, *L'Empire Peul du Macina*, I, 1818-1853 (Dakar, 1955). Jamil M. Abun-Nasr, *The Tijaniyya* (London, 1965) gives essential background for Al Haji 'Umar, and Eugène Mage, *Voyage au Soudan Occidental* (Paris, 1868) gives a contemporary account of his empire. Other aspects of this period are studied in A. Adu Boahen, *Britain, the Sahara and the Western Sudan 1788-1861* (Oxford, 1964). A major study of Samori is being written by Yves Person; meanwhile, see his articles, "Les ancêtres de Samori," *CEA*, No. 13 (1963), and "La Jeunesse de Samori," *Revue française d'histoire d'Outre-Mer* (1962).

There is a narrative account of the rise of the French West African empire in the chapters by Maurice Delafosse in Volume IV of Gabriel Hanotaux and Alfred Martineau, *Histoire des Colonies françaises et de l'Expansion de la France dans le Monde* (Paris, 1931). P. Cultru, *Histoire du Sénégal du XVe siècle à 1870* (Paris, 1910) and André Villard, *Histoire du Sénégal* (Dakar, 1943) give useful surveys of French activity in Senegal. Like other colonial histories, they contain material of much interest to African historians, without always drawing out its most interesting implications. Abdoulaye Ly, *La Compagnie du Sénégal* (Paris, 1958) is less a study of African history than of nascent French capitalism in the period 1673-96; nor is André Delcourt, *La France et les établissements français au Sénégal entre 1713 et 1763* (Dakar, 1952) truly Afrocentric. A major source for later French policy is Christian Schefer (ed.), *Instructions générales données de 1763 à 1870 aux Gouverneurs et Ordonnateurs des éstablissements français en Afrique occidentale*, two vols. (Paris, 1921, 1927). The French slave trade is studied in Gaston-

Martin, *Nantes au XVIIIe siècle: l'ère des négriers* (Paris, 1931); for its conduct in Africa, see Simone Berbain, *Le Comptoir français de Juda au XVIIIe siècle* (Paris, 1942). From his thesis on "Dahomey and its Neighbours, 1708-1818," (Ph.D. University of London, 1963), Isaac A. Akinjogbin has written "Agaja and the Conquest of the Coastal Aja States, 1724-30" in *JHSN*, II (1963).

On early nineteenth-century Senegal, the best works are still those of Georges Hardy, *La mise en Valeur du Sénégal de 1817 à 1854* (Paris, 1921), and "L'enseignement au Sénégal de 1817 à 1854," BCEHSAOF, IV (1921). The later part of the century is being studied by M. Roger Pasquier, who has published a number of articles, including "Villes de Sénégal au xixe siècle," *Revue française d'histoire d'Outre-Mer*, 168-9 (1960). Jacques Charpy has edited a collection of documents on *La Fondation de Dakar* (Paris, 1958). Among contemporary accounts P. D. Boilat, *Esquisses Sénégalaises*, two vols. (Paris, 1853), is especially interesting; the author was a missionary priest of part-Wolof descent. Two recent studies of the development of French activities down the coast are Bernard Schnapper, *La Politique et le Commerce français dans la Golfe de Guinée de 1838 à 1871* (Paris, 1961); and Paul Atger, *La France en Côte d'Ivoire de 1843 à 1893* (Dakar, 1962). On Guinea, much can still be learned from André Arcin, *Histoire de la Guinée française* (Paris, 1911), a compilation by an early administrator. Colin W. Newbury, *The Western Slave Coast and Its Rulers* (Oxford, 1961) relates the history of Dahomey to that of its African neighbors over an extended period, with uneven success. Two more general surveys are Henri Brunschwig, *L'Avènement de l'Afrique noire* (Paris, 1963) and John D. Hargreaves, *Prelude to the Partition of West Africa* (London, 1963).

There is still no proper biography of Faidherbe, but brief biographies have been written by André Demaison (Paris, 1932), and Georges Hardy (Paris, 1947). Faidherbe's own compilation *Le Sénégal* (Paris, 1889), is not easy to use. On his successors Jacques Méniaud *Les Pionniers du Soudan*, two vols. (Paris, 1931) contains important material from the Archinard papers and elsewhere, presented in "drum-and-trumpet" form. An excellent thesis on "The French in West Africa: A Study in Military Imperialism," was presented by Mr. Alexander S. Kanya-Forstner for the degree of Ph.D. of the University of Cambridge in 1965. Among the more useful of the memoirs of military travellers are Joseph S. Gallieni, *Voyage au Soudan français* (Paris, 1885), and *Deux Campagnes au Soudan français* (Paris, 1891); Louis G. Binger, *Du Niger au Golfe de Guinée*, two vols. (Paris, 1892), and Etienne Péroz, *Au Soudan français* (Paris, 1889). The two last contain accounts of Samori's empire. The motivation behind French imperialism is discussed in Henri Brunschwig, *Mythes et Réalités de l'Impérialisme colonial français* (Paris, 1960), translated as *French Colonialism; myths and realities* (London, 1966). One aspect of its methods is studied in an important work by Denise Bouche, "Les Villages de Liberté en A.O.F.," *Bulletin de l'IFAN*, Dakar, XI (1949), 491-540, XII (1950), 135-215.

Information on the colonial period must still be sought largely in the general works noted above, or in specialized articles such as those mentioned in footnotes to Chapter Eight. The only attempt at a comprehensive interpretation is the hostile one in the second volume of Suret-Canale. Useful accounts of French policy at particular points can be found in Raymond Leslie Buell, *The Native Problem in Africa*, two vols. (New York, 1928), and in Lord Hailey, *African Survey* (first published, London, 1938; revised edition for 1956, London, 1957). Robert Delavignette, *Freedom and Authority in French West Africa* (London, 1950), states the code of a liberal and humane French colonial administrator. P. Alexandre, "Le Probleme des Chefferies en Afrique Noire française," *La Documentation française*, No. 2508 (Feb. 10, 1959), provides material for a more profound analysis. An interesting contribution by a moderate Ivoirian is F. J. Amon d'Aby, *La Côte d'Ivoire dans la Cité africaine* (Paris, 1951).

On postwar developments there is a great and growing literature, consisting both of writings by Africans and of political, sociological, or economic analyses by foreigners. Kenneth Robinson, whose own articles pioneered the study of French-speaking Africa in the United Kingdom, gives "A Survey of the Background Material for the Study of Government in French Tropical Africa," *American Political Science Review*, L (1956), 179-98; John A. Ballard has extended this in "Politics and Government in Former French West and Equatorial Africa: A Critical Bibliography," *JMAS*, III (1965), 589-605. Ruth Schachter-Morgenthau's *Political Parties in French-Speaking West Africa* (Oxford, 1964) is a broad though detailed study of political activity in Africa which provides indispensable material on the postwar period. Reference may be made to its bibliography for an introduction to recent literature on the postwar period; this note lists only a small sample of recent works in English. A brief stimulating survey, now somewhat dated, is Thomas Hodgkin and Ruth Schachter, *French-Speaking West Africa in Transition* (*International Conciliation*, No. 528, New York, 1960). Michael Crowder has an admirable brief introduction to *Senegal*, 2nd ed. (London, 1966); Kenneth Robinson a rather fuller one in "Senegal: the Elections to the Territorial Assembly, March 1957," in William J. M. Mackenzie and Kenneth Robinson, *Five Elections in Africa* (Oxford, 1960). William J. Foltz, *From French West Africa to the Mali Federation* (New Haven, 1965); Aristide Zolberg, *One-Party Government in the Ivory Coast* (Princeton, 1964); and Elliott P. Skinner, *The Mossi of the Upper Volta* (Stanford, 1964) all contain good analyses of problems of contemporary history. William H. Friedland and Carl G. Rosberg Jr., *African Socialism* (Stanford, 1964), has a good bibliography. Other writings by African political leaders and men of culture may be traced through Janheinz Jahn, *A Bibliography of Neo-African Literature* (London, 1965).

For current bibliographical information, consult the *African Studies Bulletin* published for the African Studies Association by the Hoover Institution, Stanford, California.

INDEX

Abd-el-Kadr ben Mahi-el-Din (1807/8-83) Algerian ruler, 95

Abijan, 13, 118, 158

Abomey (see Dahomey, Kingdom; Fon)

Abu Bakr (d. 1087), 21

Adamson, Michel (1727-1806), botanist, in Senegal 1749-53, 69

Afrique Equatoriale Française, 4, 114-15, 145, 159

Afrique Occidentale Française, 3-4, 110, 113-62
   administrative organization, 123, 137-42

Agaja, King of Dahomey (c. 1708-40), 43-44

Agni people, 31, 90

Agriculture, 4-8, 16, 32
   in 19th century Senegal, 79-82

Aguibou, Son of Al Hajj 'Umar; ruler of Dinguiray c. 1874-93; administered Macina for France 1893-1902, 105

Ahmadiyya, 128

Ahmed Bamba (c. 1850-1927) founder of Muridiyya, 127-28

Aja people, 31, 42-44, 62, 87 (see also Fon)

Albreda, 63, 83

Alfa Ibrahima, led jihad in Futa Jalon, 1725, 51

Algeria, 85, 93-95, 100, 137
   war of 1954-62, 1, 154, 161

Ali Chandora, Emir of the Trarzas, 65

Allada, 31, 42-44, 61, 74, 109

d'Almada, André Alvares, Portuguese writer of 16th century, 30-31, 40

Almoravids, 21-22

Amadou Seydou (1928), Ambassador of Niger Republic, 53n

Amadu (c. 1835-98), son and successor of Al Hajj 'Umar, 57, 103
   relations with France, 98, 102, 110

Amoku, 74

Aniaba, Ivoirian, at French Coast 1688-1701, 41

Anomabu, 74

Arabs:
   Arabic language, 2, 16
   influence on Western Sudan, 16, 19-27

Archinard, General Louis (1850-1932) Commandant, in Sudan 1888-93, 101-2, 104-6, 111, 164

Arguin, 34-35, 60, 64-65

Army, French:
   African forces, 70, 76-77, 94, 111, 121-22, 135-36, 144, 154
   influence in administration, 105-107, 110-12, 129
   operations, 93-94, 98-105, 109, 115

Ashanti, 19, 28, 31, 32, 34, 89, 104

Askia Muhammed (c. 1443-1528) King of Songhai 1493-1528, 23-24, 27

Assimilation:
   French policy, 135-36, 139, 147
   in Senegal, 68-71

Assinie, 41-42, 61, 90

Association Policy, 136-37

Azurara, Gomes Eannes de, Portuguese chronicler of 15th century, 35

Bafoulabe, 100

Bakel, 82

Bakri, Al, Andalusian geographer of 11th century, 20-22

175